Making Your Own

BUSH KNIFE

Making Your Own

BUSH KNIFE

A Beginner's Guide
for the Backyard
Knifemaker

Bradley Richardson

FOX CHAPEL
PUBLISHING

© 2020 by Bradley Richardson and Fox Chapel Publishing Company, Inc., 903 Square Street, Mount Joy, PA 17552.

Making Your Own Bush Knife is an original work, first published in 2020 by Fox Chapel Publishing Company, Inc. The patterns contained herein are copyrighted by the author. Readers may make copies of these patterns for personal use. The patterns themselves, however, are not to be duplicated for resale or distribution under any circumstances. Any such copying is a violation of copyright law.

ISBN 978-1-4971-0012-1

Library of Congress Cataloging-in-Publication Data

Names: Richardson, Bradley, author.
Title: Making your own bush knife : a beginner's guide for the backyard
    knifemaker / Bradley Richardson.
Description: Mount Joy, PA : Fox Chapel Publishing, 2019. | Includes index.
    | Summary: ""Instructs the reader on how to assemble the tools and
    materials to prepare for forging a knife out of steel. Gives tips on
    selecting steel, building forges, heating, tempering, quenching,
    annealing, sharpening, grinding, and the other processes associated with
    creating a fixed-blade knife"-- Provided by publisher.
Identifiers: LCCN 2019033508 (print) | LCCN 2019033509 (ebook) | ISBN
    9781497100121 (paperback) | ISBN 9781607657316 (ebook)
Subjects: LCSH: Knives--Design and construction--Handbooks, manuals, etc.
Classification: LCC TS380 .R53 2019 (print) | LCC TS380 (ebook) | DDC
    621.9/32--dc23
LC record available at https://lccn.loc.gov/2019033508
LC ebook record available at https://lccn.loc.gov/2019033509

To learn more about the other great books from Fox Chapel Publishing, or to find a retailer near you,
call toll-free 800-457-9112 or visit us at *www.FoxChapelPublishing.com*.

We are always looking for talented authors. To submit an idea, please send a brief inquiry to
acquisitions@foxchapelpublishing.com.

Printed in Singapore
First printing

CONTENTS

Chapter 1: The Steel

Chapter 2: Designing & Profiling

Chapter 3: The Cutting Edge

Chapter 4: Preparing the Tang for a Handle

Chapter 5: Hardening the Blade

Chapter 6: Finishing the Blade

Chapter 7: Choosing Handle Material

Chapter 8: Attaching a Handle

Chapter 9: Shaping the Handle

Chapter 10: Proper Knife Care & Maintenance

GALLERY

Damascus blade with a black walnut and cast turquoise handle. This handle also features mosaic pins.

A drop point knife that features a high contrast handle made from maple and African blackwood.

A blade that I made myself years ago. This one features a simple oak handle and a Scandinavian grind.

This three-tone handle is made from African blackwood, cast turquoise, and desert ironwood. The blade is Damascus forged from 1084 and 15N20 steels.

The handle is made with cosmic resin and oak. This was a collaboration with Red Nose Leather who made the leather sheath.

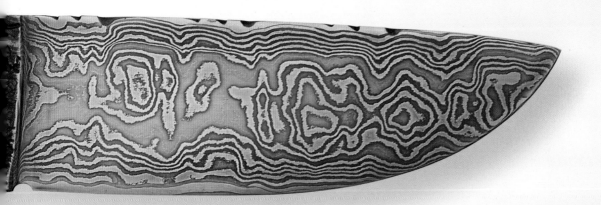

A simple bush knife made from 80CRV2 steel and a black walnut handle.

A larger camp knife that features a brass bolster in front of some desert ironwood. The pins are brass to go along with the bolster.

This handle was made from black G10 and the blade from 80CRV2.

Designed to match the above blade, this one features Jade Ghost G10 and has an 80CRV2 blade.

The handle on this knife is made from linen-based phenolic resin. The black pins are G10 material.

An outdoor knife with a three-tone handle design. This one features African blackwood, cast turquoise, and desert ironwood.

A low layer Damascus blade with an African blackwood and cast turquoise handle.

This Damascus skinning knife features a brass finger guard and cocobolo handle. The handle also includes birch bark and G10 spacers.

A set of four small matching knives. These are all made from O1 tool steel and feature Jade Ghost G10 in their handles.

This fillet knife features a leather-stacked hidden-tang handle. The handle also includes black G10 spacers and brass fittings.

This mini-cleaver has a cherry and black walnut handle.

A skinning knife with desert ironwood and cast turquoise handle.

A Damascus drop point blade that has bocote, cocobolo, and G10 in the handle.

A small Damascus knife forged to about 200 layers. The handle is made from African blackwood and desert ironwood.

A higher layer Damascus blade. This handle features desert ironwood and a small piece of black G10.

This small hunting knife has a blade made from 1095 steel. The handle is made from ebony, white G10, and burnt oak.

This bushcraft knife displays a Scandinavian grind. The handle is African blackwood, cast turquoise, and a cast marble.

A puukko-inspired blade with a handle made from African blackwood, G10, and cocobolo.

This small fighter has a handle made from cosmic resin.

A handmade knife is much more than just a tool; it's a piece of art that reflects the vision and the passion of its creator.

INTRODUCTION

Welcome to the world of knifemaking: a rabbit hole of tools, techniques, frustration, finger slices, freak-outs, passion, and pride.

To be clear, this book wasn't sent down by the knife gods. I don't have umpteen years of experience, and I will always consider myself a student to this craft. However, I feel that I've finally made it over the initial stress-hump of knifemaking and that it's my duty to help you get from point "A" to whatever-the-hell point I seemed to have made it to today.

The knife is one of humankind's first tools. Dating back to about 2.5 million years ago, the first knives were made by battering sharp flakes from stone, oftentimes used with a wooden or bone handle for ease of use. About 10,000 years ago humans figured out how to make knives from copper; move forward 5,000 years and blades began to be made of bronze. On the heels of the Bronze Age came the Iron Age. People throughout Europe, Asia, and Africa began making blades from iron between 1200 BCE and 600 BCE, depending on the region. Fast forward to modern day, where we have developed extremely tough, durable, and hardened steels that are far superior to any blade material used in the ancient past.

Not only is there an incredible history attached to knifemaking, it also stands apart from many other modern trades and art forms. My favorite part of knifemaking is just how unique every single knife can become. If I head into the shop this week and make a knife, I am 100% certain that no other knife I make will ever be exactly the same as this one. From the blade profile to the edge design, and from the handle material to the characteristics within the steel itself, the knife is one of the most customizable works of art that has ever existed.

That being said, there is plenty for anyone to learn when it comes to the craft of knifemaking.

My advice is to challenge yourself in small increments. If you cannonball into this craft, you may never make it out alive. If you take your time and learn from every mistake, knifemaking can become a rewarding and at times meditative craft.

Stone Age knife (5,400 BCE–3,900 BCE) found in Denmark

My Knife Shop PPE

- ☐ **Safety Glasses**

- ☐ **Ear Muffs**

- ☐ **Denim Jeans and Jacket**

- ☐ **Leather Boots**

- ☐ **Particulate Respirator**

- ☐ **Ball Cap**

- ☐ **Rubber and Leather Gloves**

- ☐ **Shop Apron**

Keeping yourself protected from sparks and other knife shop dangers is extremely important.

Personal Safety in the Knife Shop

As with any craft, knifemaking comes with its own set of hazards and should be approached in as safe a manner as possible. Personal protective equipment (PPE) is essential when working with power tools, dust, chemicals, or high heats. You can expect to encounter all of these when making a knife. You need to protect your eyes, ears, lungs, and skin. It's very simple to take proper precautions, and you'll thank yourself for taking the time later on in life. As a full-time maker, there's not a single day in the shop that I'm not suited up under safety glasses, hearing protection, a respirator, and protective clothing.

Eye Protection

When choosing eye protection, know your hazards and understand the available lens materials. Generally speaking, eye protection falls into two categories: safety glasses and safety goggles. For some tasks, you may also consider a full-face shield like those used for chainsaw operation.

Safety glasses and goggles are made from numerous types of lens material, and it helps to understand the differences between them.

Polycarbonate offers excellent impact and scratch resistance, is lightweight, and can offer some protection against ultraviolet rays. The downside to polycarbonate would be that its optical clarity isn't as great as NXT polyurethane or optical glass.

NXT polyurethane (Trivex) also offers excellent impact resistance, has premium optical clarity, and is lightweight. Its downside would be the higher price tag, but some would argue that having better optical clarity is worth the investment because being able to see well could help to prevent other injuries in the shop.

Acrylic lenses are often the most inexpensive. They are not very durable, nor do they have very good optical clarity, but they are resistant to solvents.

Optical lenses are choice for those who prefer prescription glasses. They often have excellent scratch resistance and offer distortion-free vision. The downside would be that they are heavier and come with a higher price tag. Generally, they additionally have poor impact resistance.

Hearing Protection

At any given time the knife shop can put off a good amount of noise. Any sounds louder than 85 decibels have the potential to cause hearing loss. Whether you're using a belt grinder, forging with a hammer, or cutting handle material with a band saw, it's important to keep those ears covered.

Earmuffs are my preference.

Earmuffs cover the entire ear and often have the capability of being attached to a helmet or face shield. They are available in many different styles and have been a preference of mine for quite some time.

Earplugs are available in a multitude of styles, such as foam plugs, silicon plugs, or universal plugs.

Foam plugs are often yellow in color and designed for one-time use. Foam plugs come with a cheaper price tag, they can irritate the ear, and when inserted using a dirty finger they pose a risk of external ear infections.

Silicon plugs are also one-time use but are made from a less irritating material. These are designed to only cover the auditory canal, and they cannot be inserted into the ear, which in turn makes it easier for them to fall out.

Universal plugs are the popular choice. These offer a layered system and completely seal off the auditory canal. Their design helps protect against sound while preventing the sense of being completely shut off.

The best footwear for the shop is a pair of all-leather boots that rise above the ankles.

Particulate respirators are what should be used in the knife shop. They are designed to capture particles in the air. The filters should be approved for at least 95 percent filtration efficiency. They do not protect against gases or vapors.

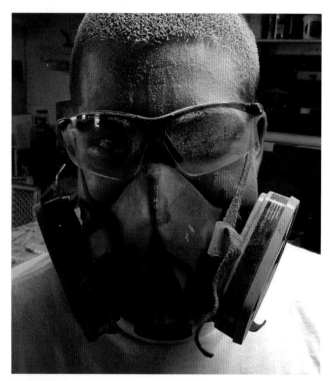

The shop can be a dusty place. Protect your lungs with a respirator.

LUNG PROTECTION

Whether you're sculpting a handle, cutting steel, or grinding bevels—anytime there is dust present—a respirator is necessary. Respirators are among the most important pieces of personal protective equipment you can use.

Leather apron, leather gloves, and a welder jacket are great to have in the shop.

PROTECTIVE CLOTHING

In the knife shop, you could be working around hot steel, hot oil, hot tools, sparks, and flames, so it is extremely important to wear clothes that are appropriate for the job. This means no synthetics or easily flammable articles of clothing. Materials such as wool, denim, leather, canvas, or 100% cotton are all safe choices of clothing. A thicker **canvas** or **leather apron** or **welding jacket** will offer some additional protection.

When working around power tools or fire, avoid baggy clothing such as loose long sleeves, hoodie strings, etc. These are all subject to being grabbed by a machine or caught by an open flame.

When you're working around fire or hot material, avoid rubber-topped boots or standard gym shoes. The best option is an **all-leather boot** that sits above the ankle.

Gloves are another great item to have in the shop. When working with epoxies and other chemicals, you will benefit from wearing disposable **rubber** or **latex gloves**. When running grinders or other machines, it can sometimes be safer to avoid gloves altogether because they carry the risk of being grabbed by belts or abrasives. When wearing gloves around machinery, it's best to choose a tight-fitting glove. When working around fire or hot metals, avoid gloves made of synthetic materials. Leather is a good choice.

Shop Safety Equipment

In addition to suiting up in PPE, you must also consider having some shop safety equipment on hand as well. I was once told to always hope for the best but prepare for the worse. I cannot stress safety enough. This may not be the most dangerous trade in the world, but caution should never be taken lightly. To make things easy, I've broken these items down into a list that I'd recommend any beginner have in their shop.

Shop Safety Equipment

☐ **Fire Extinguishers: Class A and Class B**

☐ **Dust Collection System**

☐ **Eye Wash Solution or Eye Wash Sink**

☐ **Proper Lighting—Bright LEDs are best**

☐ **First Aid Kit**

Keep Class A and Class B fire extinguishers nearby.

FIRE EXTINGUISHERS

I grew up with a firefighter dad, and because of that, fire safety has been ingrained into me. I keep three fire extinguishers in my shop (see below). Not to mention, I also have two large buckets full of water at all times that I use for cooling steel. Anyone using a forge or working around power tools and other heat sources should have a fire extinguisher on hand.

When selecting a fire extinguisher it's important to understand the different types. The most common types are classified as Class A, B, or C.

Class A fire extinguishers are effective against fires involving wood, paper, trash, textiles, or plastics. **Class B** fire extinguishers are effective against liquid fires involving gasoline, kerosene, oils, or even paints. **Class C** fire extinguishers are effective against electrical fires involving live electrical equipment. So just try to remember: Class A is for trash, Class B is for liquid, and Class C is for electrical.

I recommend keeping a Class A or a general-purpose extinguisher on hand in case of emergency. And if you're quenching a hot blade into oil (a step that I cover later on), keep a Class B fire extinguisher nearby too. Never dump a bucket of water on an oil fire. Oil has a lower density than water, meaning it will always float on top. Adding water to an oil fire will only help the fire travel. A bucket of sand or fine dirt would do a better job than water.

DUST COLLECTION

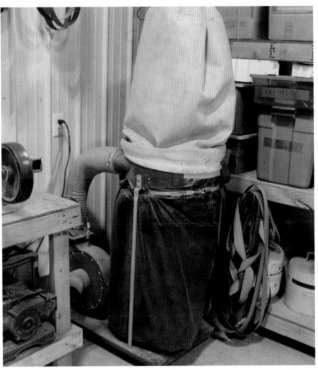

This is my dust collection system, featuring a disposable collection bag.

Dust collection devices are used near or connected to any tool that kicks up a lot of dust. I turn on my dust collector when I'm shaping handle material and it does a great job at keeping the dust level down. This helps to keep your lungs safe and saves you some cleanup time at the end of the day. Avoid using your dust collection device for both grinding metal and sanding wood. The sparks can mix with the wood dust inside of the dust chamber and potentially cause the dust to catch fire.

EYE WASH

Eye wash bottles, or better yet an eye wash sink, can really come in handy. I'm pretty adamant about wearing eye protection, but I still seem to get the occasional particle in my eye. A proper eye wash solution will be the best choice for flushing your eyes if needed.

Eye washing stations provide on-the-spot decontamination. When particles enter your eye, it's best to take care of the problem immediately.

PROPER LIGHTING

Something else that is often overlooked is proper lighting. If you can't see what you're doing, you greatly increase your chances of injury in the shop. This will also help your eyes from straining in a dark room. I recommend installing a few bright LED lights.

Tools for the Beginning Knifemaker

Make sure you've read the safety material first. If you go blind or burn your shop down, you won't get much more use out of any of these tools.

I've narrowed things down to create a very budget-friendly and modest group of ten tools that will get anybody started making knives. Many people may already find most of these tools in their home, and if not this entire list of tools can be bought new for around $150. You can always make upgrades as you move along, but these ten tools will prove their worth in any knifemaker's shop.

1. FILE

2. RASP

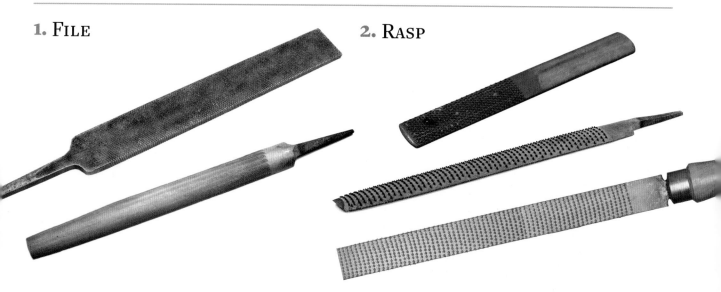

From top: Single-cut file, half-round file.

From top: Four-in-hand rasp, half-round rasp, rasp.

The first tool on the list is a file. More specifically, a **single-cut file**, also known as a bastard-cut mill file. This tool can be used for fine-tuning a blade profile as well as to form bevels. A sharp file will make fast work of soft (annealed) steel, and the use of a file card or a wire brush will help to prevent the file from clogging up during use. A file may be slower at cutting steel than a belt grinder, but it has a much lower price tag—a quality file can be bought new for around $6.

A rasp is a much coarser form of file, used to shape wood and other materials. Rasps are great at shaping most handle materials. I recommend getting your hands on a **half-round rasp**. This shape offers both a flat side and a rounded side for more versatility during handle shaping. A **four-in-hand** is also a great option. This is a combination tool that features both a half-round rasp and a half-round file. A quality rasp can be bought new for around $7.

3. FORGE

My firebrick forge.

If you plan to buy a forge, you might spend $200–$300 on a very basic model. However I'd recommend any beginner to fashion his or her own forge using firebricks and a blowtorch. I go over this in detail on pages 52–53. The price of firebricks and a simple blowtorch usually don't exceed $35. Keep in mind that the gas cylinder on a torch will need to be replaced.

If you plan to use your forge for more than just heat-treating, you may consider buying or making a forge burner and using it with a full-size propane tank. I'm recommending gas forges because they are safer in the sense that they can be shut off in a matter of seconds. They are also low-odor and non-threatening to your lungs, unlike coal forges.

4. QUENCHING CONTAINER AND MEDIUM

My quenching container. See page 108 for how to quench steel safely.

In order to heat-treat your knife you'll need a safe, metal container for quenching. It doesn't need to be huge unless your blades are huge. The rule of thumb is to use one gallon of quenching liquid per pound of steel you plan to quench. A metal paint can, a small pale, or even an ammunition box will work great for this; just be sure that whatever you use is watertight. My favorite quenching medium is canola oil and that's what I recommend to any beginner. You can pick up a small metal container and a gallon of canola oil for around $8.

Canola oil.

5. TEMPERING OVEN

No need to be fancy: even a toaster oven works for tempering steel.

A pro-quality tempering oven can cost thousands of dollars. But if you have permission to use the household oven or even the toaster oven, you're good to go. You can also use a torch to temper a blade, and if you buy one to make a little forge, you've got another way to temper a knife.

6. DRILL

A drill is a great tool for any shop, and anyone who is at all handy probably has one lying around. A drill press will always provide a more accurate hole, but a hand drill will do the trick if you need it to. A cheap little drill press may run you about $45. Hand drills can get pretty fancy, but a lower cost hand drill will run about $30 new. But that $30 can also probably get you a much nicer used drill.

7. VISE

A vise is an awesome tool to have. Anytime you're working with a handheld grinder, or a hacksaw, it is important to securely mount your workpiece into a vise. A high quality vise can fetch a pretty high price, but I've seen many used vises at a much lower price point. An average quality vise often sells new for about $40. Whether you're grinding a profile or filing a choil, it's good to know that your blade will stay in place during the process.

8. CLAMPS

A few little clamps don't seem like much, but they are very helpful in securing handle material to a tang. I'm sure you'll find many other random uses for these in the shop—I know I do all the time. A few simple clamps may run you about $12 new. In knifemaking, clamps help hold handle material together while epoxy cures.

9. SHARPENING STONE

This should be a given, but you can't call a knife complete without sharpening it. I recommend a **two-sided whetstone** that features both a low (400 or so) grit and a high (1000–3000) grit. Take good care of this stone and it will last you quite some time. High quality whetstones can get pretty expensive but you can find a simple whetstone for about $11. Be cautious about buying these used because they can develop pits or uneven sinks when they aren't properly cared for.

10. COMMUNITY!

And finally, one of the best tools that you can have is the already existing community of knifemakers. Here and there you'll run into a jerk, but for the most part the modern knifemaking community is one of the most welcoming and helpful groups of people I have ever been exposed to. Whether you're on social media or at a knife show or convention, fellow knifemakers are often always happy to answer questions to help you get to the next level. There are many different clubs within the broader community that offer a great support system for both beginner and experienced knifemakers. Get out there and soak up all the knowledge you can!

Shopping List to Get Started on a Budget

- ☐ Single-cut file for shaping steel
- ☐ Half-round rasp for shaping handles
- ☐ Blowtorch and firebricks to build a forge for heat-treating steel
- ☐ Metal watertight container and canola oil for quenching steel
- ☐ Oven or toaster oven for tempering steel
- ☐ Vise for steady sawing
- ☐ Drill or drill press for making pinholes
- ☐ Clamps for attaching handle material to steel
- ☐ Two-sided whetstone for sharpening steel
- ☐ Join the knifemaking community to get support and wisdom

Tools for the Intermediate Knifemaker

Don't think that you need fancy tools to make a fancy knife. Your patience and determination are what decide how nice your knife will be. Even if you have the money to spend, I highly recommend starting with simple tools because it's good to learn how to properly use files and other hand tools. I've upgraded my setup since I first started, but I'll never replace a trusty file. Hand tools get me out of a pinch all the time, and I'm happy that I spent the time learning with basic tools at the beginning.

> ### To many, the belt grinder is the ultimate tool for the knifemaker.

I'm a firm believer that the best tool for the job is one that you can find in the garage. I've learned a lot by working with what I have and improvising to make up for what I don't. I've built most of my own forges, both gas and solid fuel. I've built two full-size belt grinders from scratch, and restored and modified many flea market tools to save money. Used tools may not be the best tools, but fixing them up will teach you a thing or two, and that's worth more than the money you saved.

In addition to the tools I recommend in the previous section, I suggest looking for the tools described below to increase your efficiency in knifemaking.

I wouldn't even attempt to log and count all of the tools I've found to be helpful over the years. Tools such as straightedges, squares, and other measuring devices are absolutely good to have on hand. Other simple items such as tape, markers, sandpaper, oils, and epoxies will also prove their worth in the knife shop. What I've laid out here are just the common tools for both the beginner or intermediate knifemaker. You'll soon learn that these lists are only

a starting point to what is available on the market today, but these tools are more than enough to set you off on the right foot.

ANGLE GRINDER

Angle grinders are handheld grinders used to both cut and grind material to shape. The angle grinder can accept a multitude of abrasive discs used to accomplish different tasks. For more on angle grinders, turn to page 82.

A lighter weight farrier-style anvil.

ANVIL

Anvils are heavy steel or iron blocks that are used as hammering surfaces for metalworking. I go into much more detail on anvils later in the book—see page 63.

Band Saw

Band saws are excellent for cutting curves or ripping down material. These saws are great for initial wooden handle profiling and for processing handle material.

Belt Grinders

To many, the belt grinder is the ultimate tool for the knifemaker. Belt grinders are found in almost every modern knifemaking shop. These machines are most commonly used to shape blades, grind bevels, and contour handle material. These are designed to support many sizes of belts, including 1 × 30 in. (25 mm × 76 cm), 1 × 42 in. (25 mm × 107 cm), 2 × 42 in. (51 mm × 107 cm), and 2 × 72 in. (51 mm × 183 cm). I cover belt grinders in depth on pages 83–85.

Center Punch

The center punch (nail punch or nail set) can be used along with a hammer to create a divot to mark the location of a hole to be drilled in a tang prior to drilling pinholes.

A 4–5 lb. (1.8–3.2 kg) sledge flattens steel quickly.

Hammer

The hammer is an essential striking tool for those planning to forge a blade to shape. Used in combination with an anvil, hot steel can be manipulated at a fairly rapid rate. For a complete overview of hammers used in knifemaking, turn to page 60.

Disc Sander

The disc sander is an awesome tool when it comes to squaring and flattening handle material.

Drill Press

The drill press is the most popular and ideal tool choice for drilling holes. When knife handle material and pins are assembled, it's very important that the holes are perfectly aligned, and a drill press helps to guarantee that the drill bit is level.

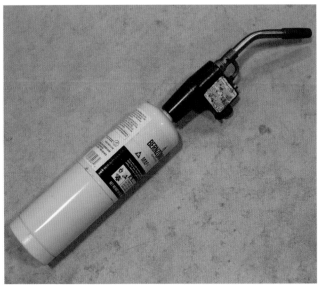

TORCH

The torch is a handy tool to have in a knife shop. It can be used to soften particular areas of a blade, as well as to temper an edge. A torch can even be used as a heat source within a smaller forge (see page 52).

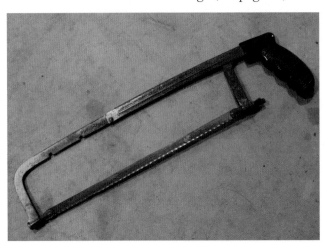

HACKSAW

Even if you have the nicest power tools on the market, the hacksaw is a great tool to have in the shop. It's handy when it comes to small tasks such as cutting pin material, and can also be used to cut away waste material from a blade.

TONGS

Tongs allow you to hold hot steel during forging operations. Tongs are a great way to keep a greater distance from the quench tank while hardening a blade—sometimes a fiery task. For more on tongs, see page 62.

Parts of a Knife

Back/Butt

Guard

Spine

Blade

Handle

Pin

Ricasso

Cutting Edge

Front/Tip

Fixed-blade knives have no moving parts and are affixed in an open and usable position. Because there are no moving parts, fixed-blade knives are considered stronger and more robust than folding knives. Of course, this depends on how the blade is made. If it has a nice profile, well executed bevels, and a proper heat treat, a fixed-blade knife is almost always stronger than a folding knife.

There are many styles of fixed-blade knives, and the differences between them refer to the shape of the tang and how it has been attached to the handle material. These different types of handle construction have their own strengths and weaknesses. Once you've gotten a firm grasp on knifemaking, it won't be long before you can use any of these techniques to create a strong and reliable handle.

On the Knife as Survival Camping Tool

A lot of survivalists will say that a knife is the ultimate "one tool option." Meaning they can use the knife to chop, baton firewood, process food, and accomplish any small feathering or cutting tasks. I'll agree and say that if I could only take one tool, a knife would be that tool. But don't think that a knife will ever replace a good quality axe or saw. Whenever I'm out wilderness camping, I always prefer to assemble a set of tools rather than try to get by with just one. Having an axe and a saw along with your knife will save your knife from quite a bit of abuse. Extra tools are also an insurance policy for when things go wrong.

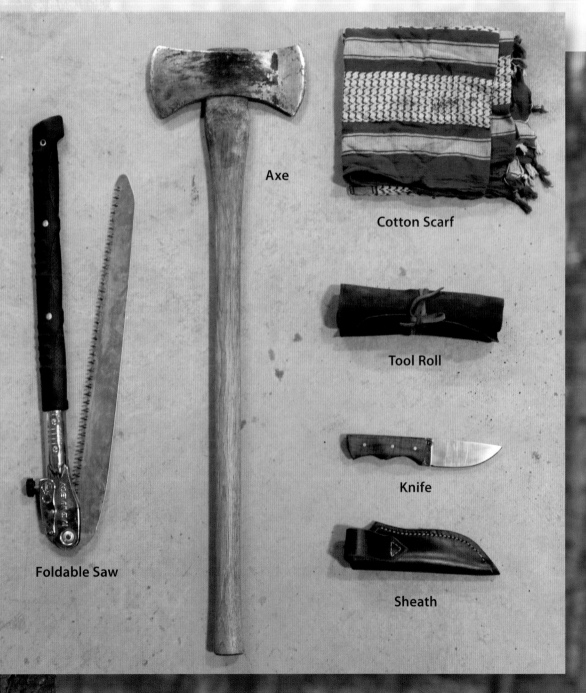

Axe

Cotton Scarf

Tool Roll

Knife

Sheath

Foldable Saw

Welcome to Knifemaking!

I'd like to be the first to welcome you into the knifemaking community. When all is said and done, have fun and be safe. Take a step into your workspace, shut out the surrounding world, and create anything that your mind envisions. Allow yourself to make mistakes, and you'll learn from yourself everyday. In this craft, hands and minds are more valuable than machines.

This is the knife that I make over the course of the book. Follow along to see the knifemaking process in action.

My Knifemaking Supplies

Some of my personal favorite knifemaking supplies are as follows:

Steels:

☐ 1084

☐ 1095

☐ 80CRV2

☐ 15N20

☐ O1 tool steel

☐ 5160

Natural Handle Materials:

☐ Walnut

☐ Oak

☐ Ironwood

☐ African Blackwood

☐ Maple

Synthetic Handle Materials:

☐ Phenolic Laminate (Micarta)

☐ G10

☐ Carbon Fiber

CHAPTER 1: THE STEEL

You can go ahead and make the most beautiful knife ever, but without the proper type of steel, you could be left with a paperweight and many hours of work down the drain. If you want a knife that will stay sharp, straight, and reliable, then it is extremely important to understand what types of steels are good for knifemaking.

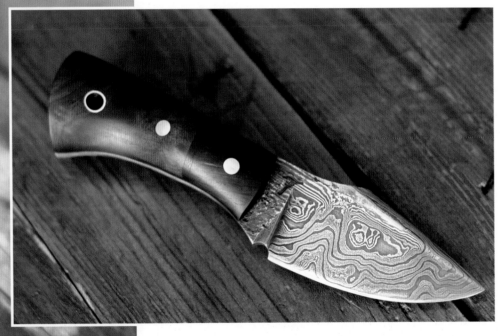

Damascus steel: the combination of high-carbon and nickel-bearing steels results in eye-catching patterns.

When choosing knife steel, you are looking for steel that is hard and tough. There's a sweet spot between these two characteristics and that's exactly where you want your steel to fall. A blade that is hard will have good edge retention and stay sharp for an extended period of time; a blade that is tough will withstand the abuse of heavy use.

Making a selection comes down to how you want your knife to perform. The steel you choose and your method of heat treatment (which I cover later on) will determine the hardness, toughness, wear resistance, corrosion resistance, and edge retention of your blade.

Steels with proper amounts of carbon are desirable to the knifemaker because the right carbon content allows the steel to be hardened. Hardening a blade provides the needed strength to survive impact and everyday use (and abuse). Using mild steel, which contains very low amounts of carbon, will result in

a poorly performing blade. When using a material such as cast iron, where the carbon content is much higher than needed, you'll again be left with a poorly performing blade.

Choosing your steel can seem overwhelming, and not just because the wrong choice may lead to complete disaster, but also because there are almost countless types of steels available.

I could write a separate book focused only on steel for the knifemaker. For this go-round, however, I'll focus on the basics—everything you need to get started with steel. I'll be categorizing knife steel into five groups: tool steel, high-carbon steel, stainless steel, Damascus steel, and recycled steel.

Take your time selecting steel. A bad steel choice can lead to blade failure and it's not worth the headache. This blade was made using 80CRV2, which is a high-carbon chrome vanadium that is extremely tough.

Buying Steel

When purchasing steel from a manufacturer it will often be available in a variety of shapes and lengths. Most commonly, you'll want to seek out flat-bar steel. This can be purchased at the desired width and thickness, saving you steps in the shaping process later on. Steel is also commonly found as round-stock or square-stock; these shapes will need to be flattened out to create a usable surface, so keep this in mind when selecting the size and shape of the steel you're buying.

*These steels are my personal favorites for knifemaking.

High-Carbon Steel

Common in survival and outdoor knives, carbon steel has proven to be sturdy and durable. It takes an edge well and sharpens easily. The downfall is that it is more prone to rust and corrosion. In my opinion, this kind of steel is the best place to start as a new knifemaker. It usually comes with a lower price tag and, with a proper heat treatment, will hold up through a lot of use.

Common Types:
1095*
1084*
1080
1075
5160

Set of knives made from high-carbon steel.

Tool Steel

The label "tool steel" represents a wide variety of carbon and alloy steels that have a distinct hardness and edge retention ideal for making tools. I've made many knives from tool steel. It can be a tough and very hard material. Even prior to hardening, I've had troubles drilling holes in tool steel without fully annealing or softening the steel. When heat-treated properly, tool steel will hold a great edge and outperform many other steels on the market.

Common Types:
D2
O1*
CPM Steels
A2

Stainless Steel

Famous for its resistance to corrosion, stainless steel is made up of carbon steel and chromium. Chromium is what provides this steel with its corrosion resistance. It's common to consider this a non-rusting steel but, in less than ideal conditions and with improper care, stainless steel will absolutely rust—think of it as "stains-less." When compared to higher carbon steel, stainless can lack toughness and edge retention. Stainless steel is commonly found in kitchen knives, folding knives, and utility knives.

Common Types:
440
440C
AUS
154CM

Damascus Steel

Damascus steel is made when multiple layers of metal have been laminated or forge-welded to create one homogenous piece. Oftentimes referred to as pattern welded steel, modern Damascus steel is generally made with the combination of high-carbon steel, such as 1084, and nickel-bearing steel, such as 15N20. The combination of these steels results in eye-catching patterns that are altered though folding, twisting, and other manipulations of the steel. The completed piece is then etched in an acid such as ferric chloride, which reveals the pattern by eating away the high-carbon steel and hardly reacting with the nickel-bearing steel.

Damascus was first produced over 2,000 years ago, with origins in ancient India. There are many different categories of Damascus steel, such as San Mai, mosaic Damascus, or canister Damascus. Making your own Damascus steel can be a very complex and time-consuming process, and it's not something I'd recommend to a beginner in the craft. It requires very accurate levels of higher forge-welding temperatures, as well as a fluxing agent to help reduce scale buildup when the billet or layers of steel are heated. This is a more advanced process that I won't go into detail here. Damascus steel can be purchased premade from some steel and knifemaking suppliers, but it usually comes with a higher price tag.

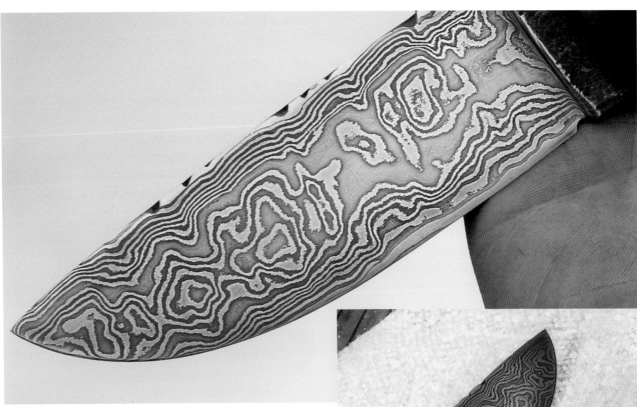

Damascus knife made up of over fifty layers of high-carbon and nickel-bearing steel.

A billet of steel prepared to be forge-welded into a piece of Damascus.

A Damascus steel blade (left) next to an O1 tool steel blade. Both are in the final stages of polishing.

Recycled Steel

High-quality steels can be expensive. This is why most knifemakers start out in the scrapyard. You can save a lot of money scrapping for steel, but you can't always be certain of the quality that you're getting. I've picked up a few tricks that are very helpful when choosing recycled steel.

MAGNET TEST

The first thing you want to verify is that your steel is indeed steel. Some alloys such as zirconium and nickel silver may come across as steel even though they aren't. A quick way to solve this problem is by using a magnet. If it sticks, then it's steel.

SPARK TEST

Now that you have a piece of steel, you'll want to check its carbon content. If it's the frame of your bike, I'll tell you now that it's probably mild steel, but if it's the chain or the gears, you may be in luck. When looking for scrap steel, keep an eye out for tools such as files or pry bars and moving parts such as axles or springs. You can check for carbon content by using the **spark test**. The spark test isn't a foolproof method, but it generally works. Steel with higher carbon content will display more forks and branches in their sparks when held to a grinder. Those with lower carbon contents will display much smaller sparks that are not as bright.

Grinding high carbon steel will result in a much brighter display of sparks that feature more branches and veins that a mild steel would.

Mild steel offers a much less impressive display of sparks.

HARDNESS TEST

The final test that I like to do is a **hardness test**. You can do this by heating the steel up to above its nonmagnetic temperature, which is around 1420°F (771°C) for most carbon steels or until it is a yellow-orange color and then quenching it into oil. You can then try cutting into the steel with a file. If the steel has been properly hardened, the file should skate off without removing any material.

You'd be surprised at how many scrap items can be repurposed into knife blades.

I've seen blades made from hand files, leaf springs, lawnmower blades, railroad spikes—you name it. Using recycled steel is a way to tinker around without losing much money on material costs. It can also be a great way to "breathe new knife" into an old piece of junk!

This knife was made from an old file.

You'd be surprised at how many scrap items can be repurposed into knife blades. Lawnmower blades and hand files will both hold a great edge when heat treated properly. Rebar or railroad spikes are hit or miss. Springs or bearings are great choices for knife steel because they are designed to flex and undergo routine pressure and movements that require the steel to be accurately tempered. I also keep some mild steels on hand that are great for practicing techniques or creating jigs.

CHAPTER 2: DESIGNING & PROFILING

"Creating a profile" is the process of transforming a piece of steel into the shape of a knife. It is in this step that you want to achieve the desired thickness and overall design that you have in mind. And it's at this point that you must choose how you will finish your knife: either by cutting away every part of the steel that isn't the knife (stock removal), or by using heat and force to mold that steel into the knife (forging).

When you see this knife at the top of the page, you'll know that the page has step-by-step instructions for making a knife.

The Design

Before you even pick up your tools, I recommend coming up with a design for your knife. Sketching out a basic profile can be helpful, because then you can reference it throughout the project to keep you on track.

The design of your knife is completely up to you, but you may want to consider the tasks that you'd like it to perform. Will your knife be used for basic woodcarving? If so, you may want a smaller blade that's easier to control. If you plan on skinning game, you may want to incorporate a drop point to the spine of the knife. Do you have plans to chop and do heavier work? If that's the case you might consider a larger blade with some forward weight.

The shape of your blade is not the only factor at play in the performance of the tool. Something else that needs to be considered is the actual thickness of the steel. Some people will say "the thicker the steel, the stronger the knife," and while that may be true in some sense, there's a fine line between a usable knife and a pry bar. A thin knife with a proper heat treat and a nice taper can withstand being bent 90 degrees or more without snapping, while a thicker knife may not have any flex at all.

Draw your design with chalk on a cement floor or the surface of the anvil.

If you are going to use the stock removal method to profile your blade, it can be as easy as drawing or tracing your design straight onto the steel. Don't bother drawing on the steel if you plan on forging your blade profile, because the ink will only burn off inside the forge, and your sketch lines would become misshapen as soon as you start molding the steel anyway. A good way to stay accurate when forging your profile is to draw your design using chalk onto a cement floor or the anvil itself rather than on a piece of paper. This way you can continuously hold your workpiece up to the design for reference without burning it up in the process.

Check out the drawings for a visual representation of some common design aspects.

Some examples of drop point knife styles.

Drop Point

Clip Point

Straight Back

Tanto

Spear Point

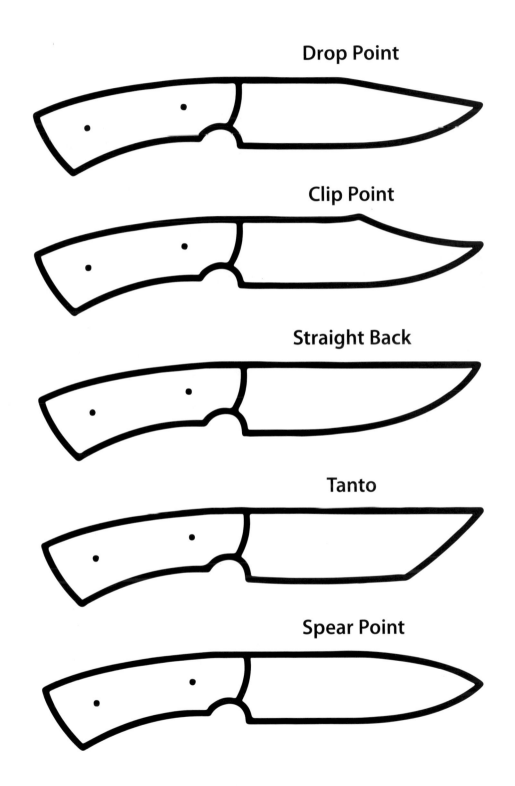

Getting Started with Forging Steel

Adjusting the gas flow valves for the propane forge.

Removing hot steel from the propane forge.

In order to shape your steel, it needs to be heated in a forge. A forge is any device used to burn fuel and retain heat; it can be as simple as a few firebricks and a handheld torch. Some of the most common types of forge fuels include propane, coal, charcoal, and coke.

EASIEST: PROPANE

Propane is a very easily accessible type of fuel, it burns clean, and it's safer in the sense that it can be shut off immediately with a valve, unlike solid fuels like coal. **It's my fuel of choice.** With a well-made propane forge, you'll be able to adjust the gas flow to help control the working temperatures. A downside to propane gas is that it can be quite pricey compared to other forge fuels. It's easy to burn through a small tank in just a day of forging.

SOLID FUELS

Coal, charcoal, and coke are all solid fuels and require an air supply to burn properly. An air supply most commonly comes in the form of a bellows and an electric blower or fan. Homemade forges may include a vacuum, hair dryer, or compressor to create a source of air.

Coal and coke are essentially the same thing, just in different states. Coke can be created by heating coal in the absence of air; this leaves behind a very high-carbon material with many of coal's original impurities burned out.

No matter what type of fuel you burn, it is important to be in a well-ventilated area. Outdoors is great, but when burning solid fuels indoors, it's crucial to have a chimney and/or extraction fan to keep your lungs safe.

HOTTEST: COKE

Coke burns cleaner and hotter than coal, but it requires more airflow to stay lit. It's generally not as smoky of a burn when compared to coal. A drawback to coke is that it sparks when burning, which can be quite painful if your hands and arms are exposed. Close attention must be paid in order to not overheat the steel in a coke forge, because it's easy to melt the workpiece if it cooks too long, and the heat can't be regulated as easily as in a gas forge.

DIRTIEST: COAL

Forging with **coal** is a traditional method. Coal burns more evenly than coke and will stay lit easier but still requires proper attention and airflow to stay alive. A major drawback to coal is that it

doesn't burn clean at all. Coke and coal can also leave behind a melted stony residue that we smiths refer to as "clinker" that has to be cleaned out of the forge after each session. In addition, burning coal releases toxic elements such as sulfur and mercury, which are damaging when inhaled.

EXPENSIVE: CHARCOAL

When using **charcoal** as a fuel source, I'd advise avoiding briquette charcoal because it is often filled with sawdust, tars, and oils that aren't ideal in a forging operation. Instead, use hardwood or lump charcoal. Some larger pieces of lump charcoal may need to be broken up a bit prior to use, but that's usually a pretty easy task. Charcoal will burn up faster than coal, generally resulting in a more expensive forging session.

Getting Started with Forging Steel **51**

How to Make Your Own Brick Blowtorch Forge

There are many ways to go about creating a forge, and each method only gets more complicated than the last. I'll go over a very simple design that many beginners use to create their first forges. The forge I'll be discussing is known as the **brick blowtorch forge**. It's constructed from high-heat firebricks and a blowtorch.

Fire bricks are always available at 4 ½ × 9 in. (11.4 × 22.8 cm). The thickness is usually either 1 ¼ in. (3 cm) and 2 ½ in. (6 cm). Either thickness will work, assuming the bricks are properly rated for over 2500°F (1370°C), but the thicker the brick is, the more heat it will retain.

1 Make sure to create your brick forge on a safe, stable surface. Avoid placing your forge on things such as wooden workbenches. Instead, consider creating a stand using metal supports or cinderblocks.

2 Stack firebricks to create a tunnel. The inside of the tunnel is where the heat will be focused and the steel placed. The number of bricks that you use will determine the size of the forge. Insulating the walls of the forge with multiple bricks is a good way to retain more heat.

3 A simple way to improve the brick blowtorch forge's efficiency is to make a door or wall to keep the heat from escaping. I prefer this wall to be removable rather than attached with cement. Having a removable wall gives you the option of heating longer lengths of steel. You can also close the forge off when working on small pieces of steel that fit completely inside the forge.

4 A hole can be drilled into one of the walls to accept the nozzle of the blowtorch. Place the nozzle into the hole and allow the body of the torch to rest alongside the forge. Creating curved interior walls using high-heat cement or by carving the brick will allow the flame to circulate through the forge and provide a better heat.

Upgrades to the DIY Forge

Using a high-heat cement or plaster will not only keep the bricks in place but also prevent heat from escaping between the cracks. This will not only create a more stable forge, but also help insulate the seams and lower the quantity of heat that escapes.

You can insulate the forge further by adding a secondary lining of vermiculite brick or ceramic wool blanketing. The goal is to retain as much of the heat as possible.

5 It might take a couple minutes for the forge to reach a proper temperature. Avoid making the forge larger than needed. A smaller opening will allow the forge to heat up faster than a larger opening.

Overview of the Knifemaking Process

By now you should have a basic idea of the tools that go into creating a custom knife. If you're lucky, you'll have a handful of these tools lying around in the garage already. We've also gone over the basics of knifemaking steel as well as some design aspects to help get you started in the right direction. Now lets jump into the techniques that you'll need to learn in order to put these tools to use.

Source the steel 39

Design your knife 47

Forge the steel into a knife 57

Clean and finish the knife 115

Temper the steel 108

Quench the steel 104

Buff the blade 119

Attach liners 140

Make a hidden-tang handle 148

Sharpen and hone the cutting edge 122

Source and design the handle 126

Make the scales 138

Profile by stock removal 76

Flatten the knife 73

Anneal the steel 75

Grind the bevels 80

Air harden the steel (alloy steel) 108

Normalize the steel 102

Drill tang holes in the handle 96

Attach the scales to the knife 154

Finish the handle 158

Finish the knife 166

Experimental Forges

A three-burner propane forge, designed with adjustable gas flow knobs.

A coke forge, featuring an electric blower and a heavy-duty fire pot or fire basin.

I built my first forge inside a cast iron grill. By lining the inside of the grill with high-heat cement, I created a bowl to burn charcoal. In the middle of the bowl I created a hole where I ran a piece of steel pipe to the outside of the grill. I then connected a vacuum that was run in reverse to create an air supply for the burning charcoal.

Thinking About Going Pro?

There are numerous professionally built forges on the market and if you plan to invest some money be sure to do your research first. You'll want a forge that is efficient and suitable for the projects you plan to use it for. If all you plan to do is create small knives, avoid getting an oversized forge because you'll only waste fuel heating it. Look at reviews and ask manufacturers to help you find the forge that best suits your needs. Some reputable companies are Majestic Forge, NC Tool Company, Pieh Tool Company, and Centaur Forge. I've owned or used products from each of these companies.

Forging the Blade

The goal with forging is to finish at least 90% of your profiling with a hammer and to clean up the last 10% with a grinder. Forging a knife, also known as bladesmithing, is an ancient practice that has survived for thousands of years. Techniques and tool preferences can vary quite a bit between smiths. I'll focus on all of the tips and tricks that I've learned to favor the most.

FIRST STEPS

Avoid steels that are more than 1 in. (25 mm) thick unless you've got a partner to help with the striking, or a mechanical advantage such as a hydraulic press or power hammer. Working alone to draw out very thick steel seems to be a modern thing. Centuries ago, smiths knew better and teamed up on bigger jobs.

If you're starting with round-stock steel, or an oddball shape such as rebar or a railroad spike, your first task is to create a flat surface and achieve the width that you want. Once you've obtained the proper width, you can focus on drawing out the steel in length until you've reached the desired thickness.

If you're using recycled steel, there's a high chance that it's not your desired width or length and it may not even be square to begin with. If this is the case, you'll need to draw out the piece of steel. Drawing out steel is a forging technique in which the workpiece is stretched at the expense of the thickness, and it's commonly done using a cross-peen hammer.

Avoid Decarburization

Leaving the steel in the forge for minutes at a time should be avoided, because overheating the steel can result in decarburization. Decarburization is the loss of carbon due to overheating, and a loss of carbon content may cause issues when hardening the blade later.

1 To properly draw with a cross-peen, you'll want to strike your steel perpendicularly down the length of the workpiece.

2 Repeat this on the other side as well. With a flat hammer or the opposite side of your cross-peen, flatten out both sides of the workpiece until you have removed your perpendicular strike marks. This process is to be continued until you've reached the thickness you desire.

3 If you want to thicken portions of your steel, you can do this by hammering the sides of the workpiece, which in turn drops the width. This is often referred to as **"upsetting the steel."** The more you do this, the more the center of the steel will start to fatten up. You'll want to be careful when hammering steel from the side, because it is easy to accidentally roll an edge or corner over itself and bury a small pocket into the steel. These mistakes are referred to as **"cold shuts,"** and they are unpleasant pits that can cause you some trouble if they are in line with your bevels down the road. To prevent cold shuts, be sure to flatten out the face of the steel each time you upset it from the side. This will remove any small fold-overs or would-be cold shuts.

Practice with Clay

When you're first learning to forge, it can be very helpful to play around with modeling clay. It molds almost exactly like steel and you can see how it reacts to pressure. It's also a great idea to find some mild steel to practice with before moving to any precious knife steel.

4 If there's anything I've picked up, it's to let the fire do most of the work. If your steel is red hot, it won't move nearly as easily as if it were yellow hot. And a good rule of thumb is to stop hammering your steel before it completely loses color, otherwise you run the risk of cracking and fracturing it.

Working Hot Steel

It's important to use a hammer that you're comfortable with. Don't start off swinging a 10 lb. (4.5 kg) hammer on your first day. A lot of experienced smiths get by using only lightweight hammers in the 2-3 lb. (0.9–1.3 kg) range. It's much easier to control a lighter hammer; without control, you can ruin your workpiece, or worse, damage your hammer or anvil. Success with a hammer comes down to your technique, where exactly you strike the steel, and how hot it is when you strike it.

WORK ON YOUR SWING

Learning to properly swing a hammer seems like a no-brainer, but it actually takes some practice. You need to practice keeping the face of the hammer square when it contacts the workpiece. You need to find a hammer that weighs enough to deliver some good force but also light enough to not immediately tire you out. The hammer should do the majority of the work for you; don't think of it as hitting the steel so much as controlling the fall of the hammer.

Scale

Scale left over on the surface of the anvil.

When forging steel you will encounter scale. **Scale** is basically oxidation that forms on the outside of hot metal. It falls off in small, thin flakes. It's better to remove this with a wire brush as you go along, rather than hammer it into your workpiece. It can cause **"pitting"**—inconsistencies on the surface of the steel—which may lead to finishing issues down the road. When Damascus steel is being forged, a fluxing agent is used to prevent scale from building up when the **billet**, or layers of steel, are initially forge-welded together. Allowing scale to form would create imperfections or de-laminations in the Damascus steel.

Setting forge welds, which is part of the Damascus process, creates a lot of sparks due to the higher forging temperatures and flux burn-off.

When you're gripping a hammer, keep your thumb either wrapped around or on top of your other fingers.

By extending your thumb along the length of the handle you run the risk of injuring your thumb in the process. To deliver sharper, more spot-on blows, grip closer to the head of the hammer. This grip sometimes requires you to put more shoulder into your technique, so find a sweet spot that's comfortable for you. When you're doing heavier work, or drawing out larger pieces of steel, it helps to grip closer to the butt of the handle. This allows the hammer more rebound, which helps to get the hammer quickly back into position for the next swing.

Beware of hammer kickback. If you have a quality anvil, it will offer good rebound, and if you miss your mark and strike the anvil instead of the workpiece, the hammer can quickly pop back up and cause injury. The best way to avoid this is to use a hammer you're comfortable with, take your time with things, and avoid placing your face directly above the workpiece.

Cross-peen hammer. If I had to choose just one hammer, this would be the one.

Planishing hammer.

Choosing Hammers

There are many different types of hammers, and when you get into decorative blacksmithing, the list grows substantially. To keep things simple, I'll be going over what I find to be some of the best hammers for bladesmithing. The hammer depends on the task you'll be performing. In bladesmithing you may encounter thick steel that needs to be drawn out, delicate tang work, point shaping, and much more.

When you're choosing a hammer, remember that it comes down to personal preference. You'll need to experiment a bit and over time you'll pick favorites. If you ever feel uncomfortable with a specific hammer, try changing your grip or move to a different weight. You'll realize pretty quickly if a hammer doesn't work well for you.

Let's start off talking about **cross-peen hammers**. If I had to choose just one hammer to use, this would be the one. Cross-peen refers to a blade-like peen that sits opposite the flat face. The cross-peen is designed to quickly draw out thicker chunks of steel by striking it perpendicularly. The sharp peen enters the steel and the excess material is pushed in either direction. The other side can be used as a **planishing hammer**, making this hammer design very popular in the bladesmithing community. A planishing hammer refers to a hammer with a slightly convex face. It's helpful to have a little bit of convex in a hammer face; this helps you avoid leaving impressions with a sharp edge or corner and ruining your workpiece. Like any hammer, cross-peens come in many different weights, and I always recommend something lighter. My first proper hammer was a 2.5 lb. (1.1 kg) Swedish-style cross-peen hammer. I still have this hammer today, but I wish I would have gone with a 2 lb. (0.9 kg) instead, because as a beginner I got really tired out using the heavier hammer.

The style of a hammer is often based on its origin. My Swedish cross-peen for example, features a cross-peen that is centered with the face on the other side.

The French version of this hammer features an offset peen the sits lower than the face. These hammer styles purely come down to personal preference and what you find easiest to use. Most cross-peens or specialty smithing hammers aren't easily found in stores, but there are many online retailers that stock them. If you're lucky, you may have a local blacksmith or farrier supply shop, and they probably have these types of hammers along with other tools such as tongs and forges. I've found many great hammers at flea markets. Sometimes they require some restoration, but if it saves money it's a win in my book.

Another very common hammer is your average **ball-peen hammer**. These offer a very nice distribution of weight and are pretty readily available at any tool store. It's not often you'll need the use of the ball-peen itself but it can add some nice texturing to a piece of material. All ball-peens are a bit different and the majority of the ones I've used have a flat striking face rather than a convex face. This means it's especially important to keep the hammer flat against the workpiece, because otherwise the sharp edges of the hammer may leave unwanted impressions.

It's nice to have a larger hammer in your collection for those days when you have some serious steel to move. I prefer a 4–5 lb. (1.8–3.2 kg) **sledge**. A sledge will often feature a flat face on either side. It's not going to draw out steel as well as a cross-peen but it'll flatten out big pieces of material pretty quickly and efficiently.

One more hammer that I'd like to mention is the **dog-face hammer**. This is an oddball and not everyone uses it, but those who do seem to love it. I've had one for a couple years now and I've found it to be very helpful when pounding in bevels on a blade. It's most commonly used as a planishing hammer. The weight-forward design makes using it resemble chopping wood. This hammer definitely requires some practice to adjust to its unique design.

It's nice to have a larger hammer in your collection like a 4 or 5 lb. (1.8 or 3.2 kg) sledge.

Dog-face hammer.

Tongs

Tongs, along with hammers, are essential to forging a blade. Tongs are made of metal and are designed to help in the handling of hot material. The long list of tong styles is overwhelming, even to me. Fortunately I've been able to experiment with many different types and I've come up with a shorter, more manageable list of tongs that will be more than enough to get you started bladesmithing. The shape of the steel you're using will determine the best tongs for the job.

Wolf jaw tongs are a good starter pair. These tongs are designed to work with a variety of stock, generally up to about 1 in. (25 mm) round, flat-bar, or square stock. If you could only have one pair of tongs, this would be an ideal choice because wolf jaws can hold about anything. Some other types of tongs will do a great job with a specific shape of steel, but wolf jaw tongs will do a decent job with many shapes of steel.

Box jaw tongs are a personal favorite of mine and do an excellent job holding flat-bar steels. The downside of box jaws is that they are designed for a specific width—2 in. (51 mm) box jaw tongs won't be able to hold a 3 in. (76 mm) bar, and 3 in. (76 mm) box jaws won't hold a 2 in. (51 mm) bar very well. I've noticed that there is about ¼ in. (6 mm) leeway between what is well secured and what is not. If you plan to work with bar stock, box jaw tongs are a fantastic choice; just keep in mind that you may need a couple of pairs depending on the size of the material you plan to work with.

U-Box tongs are a popular choice for knifemakers and I've even heard these be referred to as blade tongs. They are similar to box jaw tongs in that they are sized for specific widths and thicknesses of flat-bar steel, but they grip the steel from side to side rather than top and bottom. I've noticed this grip style to be much more secure than a top-and-bottom grip. An advantage to U-box tongs is that the pivot point of the tongs is offset from the bits or grabbing points, which allows a bypass so that you can hold the steel anywhere down the piece rather than just from the end.

From left: flat jaw tongs, wolf jaw tongs (good starter tongs), box jaw tongs (my personal favorite)

ANVILS

A good quality anvil is not cheap. Meanwhile, as bladesmithing becomes more popular, the prices on used anvils are skyrocketing. It's not often I'll see a used anvil for under $4 to $5 a pound. That's right—a used 100 lb. (45.4 kg) anvil is almost never cheaper than $400—and that's not including shipping. New anvils are even more expensive and can become quite the investment. So if your granddad has an old anvil in the back of his barn, you're already better off than the majority of beginner smiths.

When searching for an anvil it's important to avoid cast iron anvils. There's a big difference between cast iron and steel. You never want an anvil with a cast iron face. I'll say it again, **AVOID CAST IRON**.

The reason I recommend avoiding cast iron is because it's softer than your hammer. Every time you strike that cheap anvil it is going to dent and chip away, and then every time you strike your workpiece it is going to take on the shape of those dents and chips. Cast iron also provides almost no rebound for your hammer, meaning you'll have to work even harder to keep that hammer swinging.

Many times, the more affordable anvils will be the farrier's, or horseshoer's, anvils. These are lighter in weight because farriers often need to travel with them. Less weight means a lower price tag. One of my anvils is a 75 lb. (34 kg) farrier's anvil and I still use it in my shop today. Moreover the lighter weight makes it easy for me to take it to smithing demonstrations.

My advice is to look around locally and make sure that people know you're looking for an anvil. I'd avoid dropping tons of money on an anvil as a beginner; make sure you truly enjoy the craft before investing your hard-earned funds.

Find an ASO (Anvil-Shaped Object)

Something else you can do is find or create an ASO, or Anvil-Shaped Object. Most commonly a piece of railroad track (obviously don't go cut a piece of live track), or any other large piece of steel with some weight to it will do. Try to find something that is at least 50 lb. (22.6 kg).

When you finally have your anvil (or an ASO), you'll want to mount it efficiently. Some anvils may come with a metal or concrete stand, but I always recommend a wooden stand. Using a tree stump is a great option because its vertical grain will help to absorb the blows of the hammer. If you don't have a tree stump, you can do what I did and gather some 4×4s or 6×6s and arrange them into a stump formation. These can be secured with bolts or steel strapping.

An important thing to keep in mind is the height of your anvil. Some smiths prefer different heights than others, but what I've found works best is to align the face of the anvil to the position of your resting hand when you stand beside it. This way you can make use of the entire swing of your arm. With a taller anvil, you're forced to stop your swing early, and with a shorter anvil, you're left with a sore back at the end of the day.

Oftentimes you'll see the base of an anvil wrapped in chain, and I get asked about mine all the time. The chain is there to absorb the ring of the anvil. Some anvils have a very high ringing noise that can be annoying when you're spending all day forging. The chain can also aid in securing the anvil to a stand.

Forging the Point (cont'd from page 58)

5 You'll want to continue to draw out your steel until you have reached close to the desired thickness and width. Once you're happy with your progress, you can focus on forging the point of the blade.

6 Focus the majority of the heat toward the end of the material to begin forging the tip.

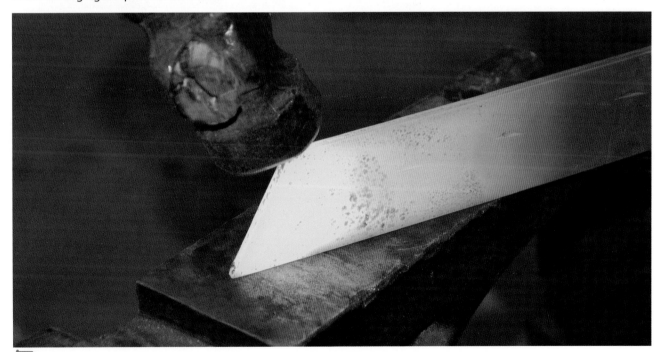

7 Begin shaping the tip by hammering in the corner.

Review: Cold Shuts & Mushrooms

Forging the steel into a point is something I struggled with when I first got started. Unless you're using round stock or a thicker material, it's easy to create **cold shuts** and **mushrooms**. An easy way to avoid making these mistakes is to use a hot chisel and cut the end of your material to an angle. You can do this by heating your workpiece and using a hammer and chisel or hot-cut tool that fits the hardy hole on the anvil to hot-cut the steel at an angle. This gives you a much easier shape from which to forge a point. This of course can be done with a grinder as well. You can then turn the hot-cut angle into a smooth curve by upsetting the obtuse angle.

A cold shut is a closed pocket that develops when the edge of a piece of steel is folded over itself; this is sometimes caused by a mushroom that has been left unfixed. When you upset steel from the side, the material that is hit will spread out under the force of the hammer, causing the steel to thicken up, or "mushroom."

An example of mushroomed steel on the butt of an axe head.

8 When you start noticing the side of the steel fattening up, lay it flat and spread out the thickness to keep it from mushrooming too much. If you strike too much onto the side of the corner rather than the blade's tip, you can end up **"fish lipping"** your material. Fish lips are a result of the steel on the outside moving faster than the steel on the inside—like a cold shut but on the side of your workpiece. If this happens you can either hot-cut or grind it out. Forging the tip isn't generally a long process once you get the hang of things. Just be patient with it and be ready to learn from any mistakes.

Hot-Cut Method Tips

Not everybody uses the hot-cut method. In fact it's more common to forge a point without the aid of a chisel, but making an initial cut prior to shaping the point can be helpful for a beginner bladesmith. Decide which corner you want to act as the point of the blade, and hammer in the other corner. Try to aim for the tip of the corner when striking. Imagine closing a bi-fold door, and that you are pushing that corner into the rest of the steel.

POUNDING BEVELS

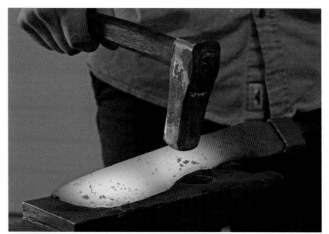

9 Beveling the edge of your blade is generally done with a file or grinder, but to save some time you can start by hammering your bevels into place. (It's optional to hammer or pound in your bevels, but I always recommend it.) This gives you an established bevel that you can use to help form the rest of the bevel later on.

10 Hammering down the entire length of the blade's edge, use your hammer at an angle rather than striking straight down. Working both faces of the edge, you'll notice the steel drawing slightly out to make a wider blade. The goal here isn't to create a sharp edge but to start your bevel. This will help you line up your grinding and save you time down the road.

11 When you are pounding in bevels, the blade will often curve backward, toward the spine, due to the remolding of the edge structure. This means that your profile has been changed and you'll have to fix it. This can be done by placing the spine of the blade on the anvil and lightly upsetting the edge until it has been bent back into place.

Profiling the Handle

12 Once you've got your point in place and your blade is starting to take shape, you'll want to profile the handle. I like to start by holding my steel on end over the edge of the anvil so that only the bladed portion is hanging off. I then make one light strike onto the spine of the blade directly over the anvil's edge so that the beginning of the handle is dented in slightly. I then use that dent as a reference point and upset all the steel on the handle side of the dent. The way you forge the handle will depend on the style of tang you are creating.

Forging a Full-Tang Handle

13 When forging a full tang knife handle, use a similar technique as you would to push in a corner or to create a point. By upsetting the side of the workpiece, push the steel inward until the length of your handle is narrow enough to be comfortable in the hand. This technique will often cause the steel to fatten up.

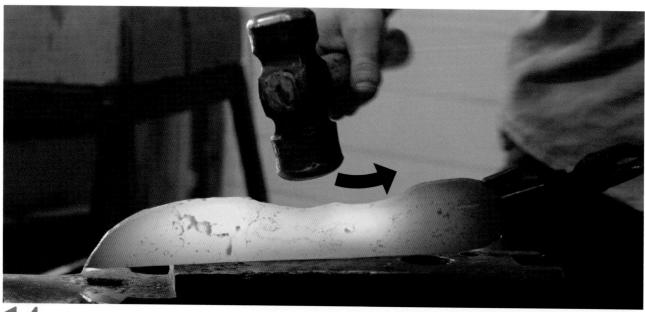

14 Remove the excess width by drawing it past the back of the handle and into any extra steel.

index finger   pinky

15 You can use the horn of the anvil to better focus your strikes and help create a more ergonomic design. Don't forget to lay your steel flat after every few strikes to remove any mushrooming. It's common practice to forge the handle section narrower at the placement of the index finger as well as the pinky. This technique will create a larger belly in the center of the handle that acts as a palm swell for a more comfortable grip.

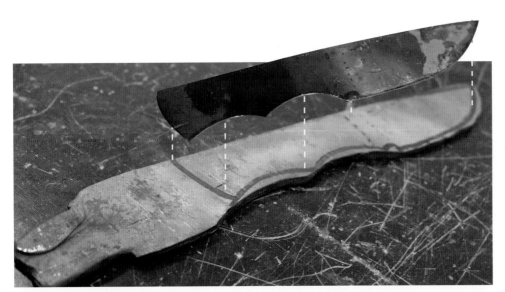

16 Once you've forged the majority of your profile to shape, you can sketch your design on the blade after it has cooled off.

17 When you have finished forging the shape of the handle, odds are you will have some excess steel hanging past the back of the handle. In this case I like to hot-cut or use an angle grinder to cut off the excess steel from the handle. Then, using an angle grinder and/or belt grinder, continue to remove any material outside of your sketch lines.

Safety Tip: Keep Hands Away from Hot Steel

Don't accidentally grab the steel to check its ergonomics, because it is most likely extremely hot. Even when the steel has lost all of its color it will be extremely hot to the touch for quite some time. Anytime I host people at my shop, I warn them about picking up just any piece of steel they see, because it can be hard to tell when it was last in the forge. I always recommend making knife templates from wood or scrap metal so that you can hold them in your hand and get a rough estimate of the comfort. I keep these templates near the anvil for reference while forging.

Let Carbon Steel Air Cool

When forging carbon steel it is incorrect to cool it quickly with water; this can cause the steel to harden, or worse, open up cracks, resulting in a faulty blade. It's best to set down the steel and allow it to cool naturally.

Forging a Hidden Tang Handle

To forge a hidden tang handle, the tang needs to be dropped drastically in width to form a narrow, tapering stick. The stick needs to taper in both width as well as thickness. The tang will need to be inset from the top as well as from the bottom of the material. Upsetting each edge and pushing them together into the center of the material will accomplish this. I rotate between upsetting the top and the bottom to keep even results.

To start forging the tang, place the handle portion of the steel onto the anvil, allowing the rest of the blade to overhang. Start striking and upsetting the edges of the material over the very edge of the anvil. This will cause a corner or shoulder to develop, separating the handle tang from the rest of the blade. Once this separation has been established, the material on the handle side needs to be drawn out past the back of the

handle. Draw it out by continuously rotating and upsetting the steel. After major progress has been made, focus more attention on the back of the tang to create a gradual taper up toward where the tang meets the shoulders.

The tang should be made to run at least more than halfway through a handle, but it may need to extend just past a handle, depending on the handle's construction. Many hidden tang handles are secured using a pin. These pins often vary in width from ⅛ to ¼ in. (3–6 mm) and require a matching hole size to be drilled into the tang. If you plan to secure your tang with a pin, make sure it is wide enough to accept a drilled hole without becoming too thin on either side of the hole. Pinholes are often placed no closer than ½ in. (13 mm) from the junction of the shoulders.

FLATTENING

I eyeball the spine of the blade against the anvil to achieve flatness.

Flattening tool, designed to be struck from the top with the work piece underneath.

18 Using a flattener (see above) and anvil, flatten the blade. This is a flat tool that is struck with a hammer to flatten steel beneath it. A flattener not only helps to straighten blades, it also helps compress and slightly drop the thickness of a blade. This can be helpful if you have small pits, hammer marks, or imperfections on the face of the blade that you'd like to repair. It's helpful to pair the flattener with a nice flat anvil as well. I use a flattener along both faces of the blade. I eyeball the spine of the blade along the flat edge of the anvil to help achieve a flat blade.

Make Your Mark

19 At this point your steel should be looking pretty close to a knife. This is also the stage where I like to incorporate my maker's mark. I hot-stamp my maker's mark into the ricasso area of the blade. The ricasso is the unsharpened part of the blade, between the handle and the cutting edge. Makers' marks can also be etched using an electro-etching tool, but a hot stamp will provide a deeper and longer-lasting impression. After hot-stamping I verify that the blade is still straight before taking the next steps.

ANNEALING

It's very important to anneal your steel at this stage. **Annealing** is the process of heating your steel and allowing it to cool very slowly. This in turn reduces stress and hardness, making the steel softer and more workable.

20 Many smiths will heat up their blade and leave it to cool down inside the forge. This is best done in a gas forge because the blade is still visible, unlike in a solid fuel forge where the blade may get overheated or even melt without your knowing. But I prefer to cool the blade in a dry medium such as powdered charcoal, sand, ashes, or, my favorite, vermiculite. Filling a metal bucket with any of these substrates and slowly plunging a heated blade into the center will force it to cool down very slowly. Be sure to bury the blade completely and you'll be able to soften the edge as well as the handle. This will make drilling pinholes and grinding bevels much easier in the later steps.

Alternative to Working Hot Steel: Profiling by Stock Removal

Stock removal doesn't require the skill level and patience that forging does. The downside of stock removal is that you're limited to the steel you can use. You'll want to begin with flat bar steel that is wide enough and long enough for the desired blade shape. If you order knife steel, it generally comes pre-annealed, meaning it will be soft enough to cut and drill with ease.

Bringing new life to an old saw blade. A plasma cutter is used to cut out knife blanks that will later be refined with a grinder.

1 Trace a design onto the steel.

2 While you can use a number of tools for the stock removal process, I'd recommend starting with a hacksaw or an angle grinder with a thin cutoff wheel. Having access to a vise will make life easier because the vise will be able to hold your material secure as you cut it. A steel band saw is another great tool for this process. Some knifemakers opt to have their knives water jet-cut or machine-cut, but these methods can be expensive if you aren't making all that money back right away.

3 Once all of the major cuts have been made, files are great for cleaning up a profile. Use single-cut flat and half-round files. Belt grinders and rotary tools are also great options for this task. It's a good idea to keep a water pail handy because your workpiece can easily become too hot to touch and you'll want to dip it to cool it off frequently.

Alternative to Working Hot Steel: Profiling by Stock Removal

CHAPTER 3:
THE CUTTING EDGE

Once you have completed shaping the profile of your knife, it's time to give it a sharp edge. We start with the bevels. The bevels are what make up the cutting edge of the blade and determine how well the knife will function.

Grinding the Bevels

To form the bevel on a knife, an abrasive is used to remove material until the desired profile is reached. Most often, this abrasive takes the form of a belt grinder. This option is popular because it allows the knife to be firmly grasped with both hands. This is unlike using a hand file or an angle grinder, both of which require the knife to be secured into a vise or clamped to a work surface. I've noticed that being able to keep both hands on the knife often results in cleaner and more precise bevels because you can see and feel the material being removed from the workpiece. However I cover all of the options in detail below.

HAND FILES: THE AFFORDABLE ALTERNATIVE

When I first began making knives, I used a variety of single-cut files to make my bevels. Files are a much more affordable option than a belt grinder (my preferred tool for this task). While files can be purchased at almost any flea market for close to nothing, make sure they are sharp.

Hang On to Old Files

The nice thing about files is that they often serve as great knifemaking steel. So hold on to old files—they can be transformed into knives when you're through with them. Keep in mind that hand-filing steel takes a lot of time and patience (both of which should be at your disposal anyway if you plan on making knives).

Helpful Tool: File Guide

A file guide is an awesome little tool to have in the knife shop and offers a number of different uses. It is often made from hardened steel or carbide and can be clamped onto a workpiece. First and foremost, this tool is used to help in filing the junction between the tang and the ricasso of a hidden tang knife, creating extremely square and even shoulders. When using this tool you can file away at your workpiece until you've reached the file guide, which is hardened material that won't be easily eaten by a file. When fitting a handle onto a hidden tang knife, it's extremely important to create square shoulders, because otherwise you'll be left with unpleasant gaps. File guides also ensure clean plunge lines when grinding bevels with a belt grinder (see page 87).

ANGLE GRINDERS: THE VERSATILE OPTION

Another tool that can be used to create bevels on a knife is the angle grinder. The angle grinder is also more affordable than the belt grinder. In addition, it has many uses outside of creating bevels.

Anytime you are using a handheld power tool, it's best for your knife to be secured with a clamp or vise. You don't want to let your workpiece shoot across the room because it's not secured well—especially when your workpiece is a knife blade!

Before using an angle grinder you will need to understand some of the different discs that can be used with the tool. **Cutoff discs** are thinner wheels that are great for stock-removal knifemaking. The thinner the wheel, the faster it will generally cut.

Grinding discs are often the same basic shape as cutoff discs but much thicker. Grinding discs aren't made for cutting through material but rather for shaping edges and corners. **Flap discs** are quite different from other angle grinder discs: they are made from a series of overlapping pieces of sandpaper. Flap discs are often used to clean up welds, rough surfaces, and sharp edges, but they can also create bevels on a knife. Flap discs are available with many different styles of sandpaper attached, although I highly recommend using ceramic flap discs. Ceramic paper makes fast work of steel and holds up longer than many other styles.

Flap disc.

The angle grinder should be paired with a vise.

Cutoff discs.

Grinding discs.

BELT GRINDERS: THE BEST OPTION

Using a belt grinder to make knife bevels is by far the most popular option. Typically knifemakers start off with a 1 × 30 in. (25 mm × 76 cm) belt grinder machine. These are fantastic little machines to have in the shop, and in fact I myself started off with a 1 × 30 in. (25 mm × 76 cm) and have made countless knives with it. I've since built my own machines but still find a use for it in the shop all the time.

Belt grinders come in many sizes, most commonly 1 × 30 in. (25 mm × 76 cm), 1 × 42 in. (25 mm × 107 cm), 2 × 42 in. (51 mm × 107 cm), and 2 × 72 in. (51 mm × 183 cm), and all of these are great for knifemaking. Typically grinders are used in a vertical position and you push the blade forward into the belt, keeping the blade at the desired angle, to create a cutting edge. What you want to look for in a belt grinder is a flat platen and a work rest. These features combined with one another with help to make grinding bevels much easier.

Serious knifemakers commonly use 2 × 72 in. (51 mm × 183 cm) machines due to their versatility. With a lot of 2 × 72 in. (51 mm × 183 cm) models, you can swap out different-sized contact wheels, platens, and other parts to help grind specific areas of your workpiece. More advanced machines often include a variable speed motor, which can be very handy. I prefer to run a lower speed when polishing or using higher grit belts.

Step Up with Confidence

When grinding bevels, it's important to approach the task with some confidence. You need to step up to the grinder and tell yourself that you are going to do a killer job. If you're uneasy about the task, there's a higher chance that you will not end up with a good result. Even if you're new to grinding bevels, talking yourself up and having some confidence is extremely helpful.

Belt Selection

This 4 x 36 in. (101 mm x 91 cm) belt grinder has been extended and redesigned to use 2 x 72 in. (51 mm x 183 cm) belt sizes.

Abrasive belts are either open or closed coat. The difference between the two is the amount of abrasive on the surface. Open coat has less and closed coat has more. Belts with less abrasive coverage won't clog up as quickly as those with higher abrasive coverage. **Closed-coat belts** are better suited for metal.

Most often knifemakers will start off using **alumina oxide belts**. Alumina oxide belts are lower budget belts that are more suited for woodworking. They can be used for grinding steel, but they are not an ideal choice; they are a very thin and flexible and will often clog up pretty quickly. However, I find alumina oxide belts to be useful when shaping and sanding most handle materials.

Ceramic belts will outlast several alumina oxide belts. They can be as hard as diamonds and are well worth the extra cost. I use ceramic belts for just about all of my steel-grinding tasks, whether I'm profiling a blade or grinding the bevels.

Alumina zirconia is a harder material and is used in higher quality belts. They are also referred to as "zirc" belts. Like ceramic belts, they are also recommended for steel grinding.

It can be harder to find specialty belts for machines smaller than a 2 × 72 in. (51 mm × 183 cm), though the belts I've mentioned above are often available for most machine sizes.

My Belt of Choice

I prefer to use a very aggressive belt when I first start beveling a knife. My belt of choice is a **36 grit ceramic belt**. I will generally complete about 90% of the bevel using a 36 grit belt. When there is a lot of material to be removed, a coarser belt will not only make faster work of the material reduction, but it will also heat up your workpiece slower than a finer belt. This is because, with the use of a finer belt, more tiny pieces of abrasive will be in contact with the workpiece, creating more friction and therefore heating it up. A coarser belt has larger abrasive pieces that are more spread out, ultimately leading to less friction against the workpiece. When removing heavy amounts of material with a fine belt, you'll have to stop constantly to dip the steel into water, otherwise it will be too hot to handle.

A high-performance ceramic belt. The "CN 466" belt series is available in grits 60 through 240.

Beveling Jigs

You can make your own jig by cutting a piece of wood to match the bevel angle you want.

When you're just getting started, beveling a knife can be a frustrating process, it can take a lot of time and practice before you really start to see the results that you want. It's common to get the hang of things with the use of a beveling jig. This is a device that works to lock the blade at a specific angle. The device is then pulled back and forth across the table of the grinder, maintaining the proper angle as you grind bevels into the knife. You can make your own jig, and it can be as simple as cutting a block of wood to match the angle you want and then holding your blade against it as you grind the bevels.

A really important aspect of grinding is to learn sensitivity to the belt, and to be able to really *feel* where the bevel is in order to keep it flat against the belt. While some smiths might call a beveling jig "training wheels" for a knifemaker, it's great if you're having trouble making bevels, but it's also important to step away from time to time to build up the feel of freehand grinding. A good practice can be to establish the angle of your bevels using a jig, and once you're about halfway through, finish things off freehand now that you have a reference point to work off of.

SCRIBING A LINE

A great way to guarantee your bevels are meeting evenly in the center of the edge is to scribe a line. If you give yourself a reference line prior to grinding the bevels, you'll be able to more easily check your progress along the way.

21 A common way to scribe a line along the edge of the workpiece is to first coat it in layout fluid. Layout fluid is most commonly blue in color and acts as a dye for your steel. An alternative option is a Sharpie marker.

22 Once the dye has been applied to the edge in which your bevels will meet, you can scribe a line perfectly down the center of the edge. Use a drill bit that is the same thickness as the edge you are scribing. Using a style of drill bit such as a brad point offers a sharp, pointed center that makes for an ideal scribing tool. Scribing the edge of the workpiece is best done on a clean, flat surface.

The Plunge Line

When initially starting to grind bevels on a knife, you need to determine where exactly you want the bevel to begin—in other words, how far from the tip of the knife the bevel will start. **Plunge lines are the starting point at which the bevel meets the ricasso.** The junction between the ricasso and the plunge line might be very sharp and straight, angled, or curved, and it all depends on the tools and techniques used to create the bevels.

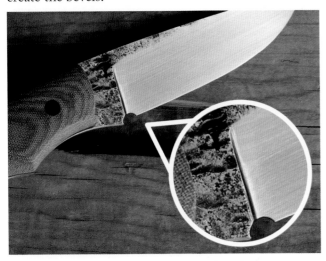

A plunge line is the starting point to a bevel. This is where the steel transitions from flat surface to ground bevel. A file guide (see page 81) will help you grind a square plunge line.

A file guide can be used to help establish clean plunge lines.

To execute a proper plunge line, make a mark on the side of the steel that can be referenced from either side. Establish the plunge line by using your mark as a starting point when you begin grinding. As you grind the bevels, continuously return to the plunge line mark without passing over it and it will slowly become more defined. Like anything in knifemaking, creating good quality plunge lines is a skill that takes practice to get good at.

A belt grinder or file can produce really clean plunge lines. An angle grinder, on the other hand, will not easily produce clean plunge lines due to its round disc. It's important to make your plunge lines symmetrical from one side of the knife to the other, so remember to follow your mark and take your time.

If you're using a belt grinder, you can adjust the tracking to cause the belt to hang over the edge of the platen by about ⅛ in. (3 mm) to create soft, curved plunge lines. Hanging the belt ¼ in. (6 mm) off the platen will result in a much rounder plunge line profile. And if your blade is angled from tip to butt while grinding, your plunge line will also be angled. This is not necessarily a bad thing; just keep in mind that if your blade is held level to the belt, your plunge line will be straight.

Ceramic grinding belts really dig into the steel; by using one you can more easily achieve a sharper plunge line. An aluminum oxide belt works better to create sweeping or curved plunge lines due to its softer, thinner design.

Choosing between a soft or sharp plunge line is completely up to you as the maker; neither has an advantage over the other. As long as your plunge lines are created evenly, you'll be in good shape. Just keep in mind that hand sanding or polishing later will be much easier if you have used a soft or more rounded plunge line. Hand sanding into the tight corner of a sharp plunge line takes more time and patience.

Bevels and Micro Bevels

Bevel Styles

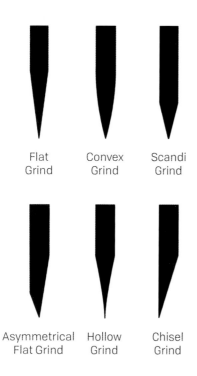

Flat Grind

Convex Grind

Scandi Grind

Asymmetrical Flat Grind

Hollow Grind

Chisel Grind

Bevel Aspects

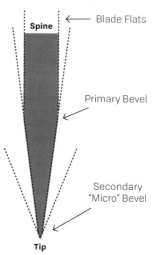

There are many different styles of bevels, and they all have their own advantages based on how the knife will be used. The most common bevel style is unmistakably a **flat grind**. This simple style of grind comes in a couple of different varieties. The first is a **full flat grind**, which translates to the edge being tapered all they way to the spine of the knife on both sides. This creates a very sharp, thin edge but is not very durable and is often only found in chef knives.

The second variety of the flat grind bevel style is a **high flat grind**. A high flat grind offers an edge that is tapered up toward the spine of the knife but stops shy of reaching it.

A bevel can be strengthened by adding a secondary bevel or "micro bevel" to it. A micro bevel is a secondary edge with a wider angle that's added to the bottom of the primary bevel. The wider angle gives the knife better edge retention because the edge is not as thin, and is therefore less prone to chopping or rolling over.

If you plan to add a micro bevel, the primary bevel cannot be tapered to a sharp edge because it is the micro bevel that will be creating the sharp edge. It's good to leave about a 0.010–0.015 in. (0.25–0.38 mm) thickness at the end of the primary bevel on a standard outdoor knife, and use that as the basis for the micro bevel. A kitchen knife might be left with about a 0.005 in. (0.13 mm) edge thickness prior to adding a micro bevel, and a heavier-use knife might be left with closer to a 0.025 in. (0.63 mm) edge thickness.

> **When you grind your bevels, you'll want to stop just before you reach a sharp edge.**

A micro bevel is often applied after the heat-treating stage, which we'll go over later on. If the blade is too thin, you run the risk of cracking or warping the blade during the quenching stage. The outer sections of the steel will also lose some carbon content due to oxidation when it's red hot later on, so it's best to leave some meat on the bevels and remove excess material during clean up, after the heat treating has been completed.

This blade features a "Scandi," or Scandinavian, bevel style.

This blade features a flat bevel style.

Top: Flat bevel style. Bottom: Scandi bevel style.

Grinding Techniques

23 When grinding bevels, I recommend always starting at the plunge line and then working toward the tip, making as many passes on the grinder or abrasive of your choice as needed.

24 Starting off with a shallower bevel angle during the initial few passes gets things started. After establishing a smaller shallow bevel, it can be used as a platform to create the rest of the bevel. Adding more pressure toward the spine will allow you to grow the bevel from the edge to the spine of the blade. Putting more pressure toward the edge of the blade will allow you to thin out the edge.

25 When you start to visibly see the bevel taking shape, you can apply more pressure to different areas of the blade in order to smooth things out where needed. Focusing more pressure into a specific area is as easy as pressing your thumb onto the bevel opposite the belt, or carefully angling the blade when needed. Be careful of angling the blade from left to right, as you may run the risk of allowing the edge of the grinding belt to cut channels into your bevel that can be hard to fix. By angling the blade like this, it is sometimes helpful to grind larger bellied areas as well as tips.

26 You'll want a water pail set up near your grinder to constantly dunk your blade into while grinding so that when it gets hot it can be cooled off.

Wear gloves made of a tighter fitting material, because loose material can be grabbed by the belt and cause injury. You may catch your fingers on the grinder from time to time, but that's a lot better that getting your hand sucked into the contact wheel because of loose-fitting gloves.

27 After completing about 90% of the bevel using a coarser belt (my preference is a 36 grit ceramic belt), switch to a medium grit, such as an 80 grit ceramic belt, to grind another 5 percent of the bevel. This will help to remove any larger scratches or grind lines made by the coarser belt. Once the previous grind lines have been cleaned up and they are uniform again, move up to 120 or 150 grit for the completion of the bevel. This will offer a good finish prior to heat-treating. Final polishing of the edge is done in a later stage of the knifemaking process. It's important to get a high enough polish (80–220 grit) prior to heat-treat because cleaning up coarse grind lines after the blade has been hardened can be quite a hassle. Very coarse grind lines have also been known to open up into cracks during the quenching stage, but this is most common in very thin blades.

CHAPTER 4: PREPARING THE TANG FOR A HANDLE

At this point, your blade has been profiled and the bevels have been ground. Soon the blade will be ready for hardening, but before that, it's helpful to prepare the tang for receiving a handle. Even before that, though, it's important to understand the different types of handle construction and the different styles of tang.

Full-Tang Knives

The full-tang blade has always been my go-to style of handle construction, and I don't expect another to become more highly requested by clients.

In this style of handle construction, the entire tang takes the shape of the handle and fills it out completely. The handle is comprised of two separate pieces of material, referred to as "scales," that are attached to either side of the tang. The method of attaching these scales varies, but it most commonly consists of metal pins that run through the tang and into the scales on either side. Epoxy is frequently used for additional strength.

Oftentimes referred to as the strongest style of handle, the full-tang design is found in blades used for hunting, camping, military use, wood processing, and anything that requires heavy work. This is not to say that other types of tang construction won't perform well at these tasks; it's just that the full tang is the most popular choice. A full-tang knife adds better balance to a larger blade and improves overall leverage. It may be a heavy choice of material for a thinner, lightweight blade, but excess tang material can be cut out in order to drop the weight.

Full-Tang Knife

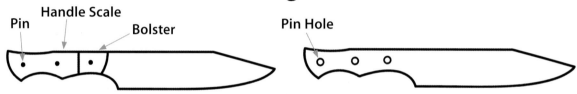

Pin   Handle Scale   Bolster   Pin Hole

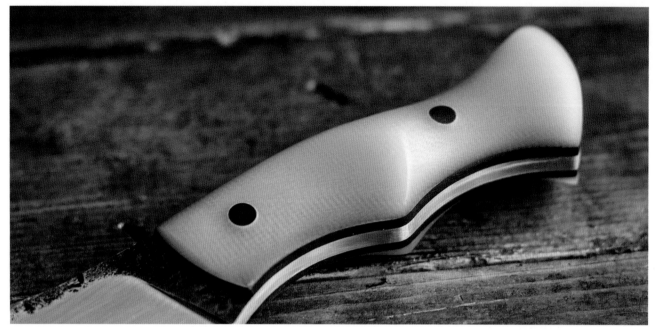

The tang takes the shape of the handle, filling it out completely. The handle is secured with pins and epoxy.

Hidden-Tang Knives

The remainder of the fixed-blade knives falls into the category of hidden-tang blades. This type of tang has been shaped into a thin tapered stick of material so it can be "hidden" in the handle. With a hidden-tang blade, the tang itself is encased in the handle, although it is sometimes visible at the butt of the knife, for the purpose of being peened over like a rivet, to act as a clamp for added handle security.

From ancient times until fairly recently, almost all knives and swords were hidden tang.

Hidden-tang knives have the advantage of being much lighter than full-tang knives. The hidden-tang handle also offers a cleaner showcase of handle material on all four sides of the handle, without the obstruction of multiple pins or a visible knife tang that would be seen in a full-tang handle.

Through general day-to-day use, a hidden-tang knife will serve its purpose, but when things are pushed to the extremes I would personally prefer a full-tang knife for added strength.

The tang is often secured with a single metal pin and epoxy, but can also be secured with the use of a pommel, aka butt cap. A **pommel** is a knob that is secured to the butt of the handle by drilling and peening, or drilling and threading, to fit a matching threaded tang. It may seem that this would make for a very weak construction, but when done properly it performs well.

There are a few things to keep in mind when creating a hidden tang if you want good results.

- The tang should taper in both width and thickness slightly from the blade side down to the end of the tang.

- The shoulders where the tang meets the ricasso shouldn't be too wide.

- The corners of the shoulders should slightly round rather than end at a sharp angle. Sharp corners won't do as well under pressure as rounded corners, and with a hidden-tang construction, the shoulder of the tang is often the weakest point.

- It's your best bet to create a close to finished tang profile prior to heat treat. Tampering with the steel after heat treat will be difficult because the steel has been hardened, and reheating the steel may compromise the blade's temper.

- Be sure to drill tang holes for pins now, as the steel will be difficult to drill after the next step.

Hidden-Tang Knife

Pommel — Handle Block — Pin — Spacer — Guard

Pin Hole

Drilling Tang Holes

Another step that I struggled with as a beginner was drilling pinholes. This is the process of drilling holes into the tang, which will be used to secure the handle to the tang with pins. Using pinholes is a very common practice and is definitely recommended on full-tang knives. They are often used in hidden-tang knives as well, but not always.

Here are some key tips to drilling holes in steel.

A. Make sure you've got the correct type of drill bit. I recommend **cobalt bits**, but you can also usually get away with carbide bits or any drill bit that is rated for drilling steel.

B. The softer your steel is, the easier it will be to drill. This is where properly annealing the blade (see page 75) can make a big difference.

C. Choose hole locations that won't sacrifice the integrity of the tang. For example, if you're working with a hidden-tang design and your tang is only ½ in. (13 mm) wide, please don't put a ⅜ in. (10 mm) hole in the center. This means you would only have ¹⁄₁₆ in. (2 mm) on either side, and that is not enough to support the tension or torsion of a knife.

D. Avoid placing a pinhole near the very edges of where your handle material will sit. Pinning a piece of wood ⅛ in. (3 mm) away from the edge will result in a very weak spot that is likely to chip away due to lack of support.

E. Use **cutting oil** as a lubricant and coolant for your drilling. It can also help to flush the metal chips away as you drill. I'd recommend cycling different cutting oils over time to figure out which one works best for you. Often one or two drops of oil per hole drilled will be plenty.

F. Use a lower drilling speed. It's harder to control speeds on a hand drill but if you have a drill press I'd recommend setting the speed to somewhere between **350–500 RPM**. You'll want to take it easy with the pressure and let the drill bit do the work.

G. It's wise to **chamfer** every hole. If anything is slightly misaligned in the handle assembly process, the chamfers work as ramps to help the pins find the holes. Holes can be chamfered with a step-bit or by simply partially drilling the hole with a larger drill bit. The pins can also be chamfered to improve ease of entry, but we'll go over pins later on when the time comes for handling.

H. Before you drill any holes, be sure to double-check your drill bit size against the size of the pin material you'll be using. This helps to prevent errors and mix-ups. As always, take your time and keep safety in mind.

I. Extra holes can be drilled to help drop the weight of a tang. This is commonly done on full-tang knives. Extra holes not only drop the weight, but also act as openings for excess epoxy to sit and helps in the bonding of handle components.

28 When drilling holes, it helps to first use a center punch to mark your holes. This allows the drill bit to easily start drilling rather than wobble around on the flat surface, looking for grip. A center punch is also a great way to verify that your steel is indeed soft enough to drill; if the tip of the center punch breaks off or hardly leaves an impression, just know that a drill bit will do the same thing. If your steel is too hard, go back and anneal the steel before drilling holes. I can't tell you how much I've suffered trying to drill into hardened steel, or how many fresh drill bits I overheated immediately.

29 Keep your blade secured with either a clamp or a vise. Sometimes when drilling steel, a drill bit can catch itself on a chip in the hole, which clogs its progress and forces the blade to start spinning dangerously on the drill bit. Keep in mind that at this point, the blade has already been beveled, so it has the potential to be sharp. To avoid a spinning blade of doom, please make sure to secure it before drilling!

CHAPTER 5: HARDENING THE BLADE

When considering the sharp point or very fine edge that many knives have, it's hard to imagine that it can withstand the forced impact, prying, jabbing, and all the crazy tasks thrown its way. What makes the steel strong and capable is the heat treat that it's given. This is the part of the knifemaking process that I like to imagine is when the blade receives its soul.

Normalizing

Before plunging a hot blade into oil to harden it, it is important to normalize the steel first. **Normalizing** is a process that resets and redistributes all of the ingredients in the steel to a uniform, or normalized, state. It also relieves stresses inside the steel caused by hammer or tool working in the earlier processes.

Normalizing should generally always be done prior to quenching. This is an especially important step to take if the blade has been forged to shape rather than ground through the stock removal process, because forging upsets the grain structure within the steel. It's a very simple step to take, and skipping over the normalizing process can result in a faulty blade. A blade with a messy grain structure is more prone to breaking during use. When a blade snaps, you can often examine the quality of the grain structure inside, and cracks or imperfections are generally noticeable as darker marks or spots.

Generally speaking, depending on the type of steel, heat the blade to 1500°F–1600°F (815°C–871°C) and then allow the steel to cool in still air until all of the color has left the blade. This is an easy way to reset the grain structure of a blade.

Judging the exact temperature of the steel based off of color alone can be a bit tricky, but using a magnet makes things much easier. Steel becomes non-magnetic at about 1425°F (774°C), so if you reach that temperature make note of the color of the steel because that can be used as a reference in the future.

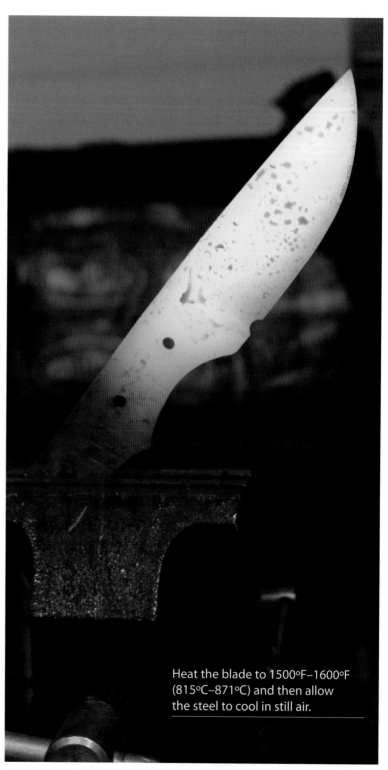

Heat the blade to 1500°F–1600°F (815°C–871°C) and then allow the steel to cool in still air.

30 Reach non-magnetic temperature and then continue to soak in the heat for a few more seconds to reach 1500°F–1600°F (815°C–871°C)—a proper normalizing heat. But stop there: if the blade is overheated, it can lead to grain growth in the steel, which could cause cracking during the quench. When heating the blade, move it back and forth in the forge to create an even heat throughout the blade.

31 Often, after I've heated up the blade to a proper temperature, I will place the very back of the tang in a vise and allow it to sit until all of the heat colors have left the steel. A simple trick is to do this in a darker area to more easily judge the color loss in the steel. Repeat this process two to three times to help equalize the grain structure inside the steel.

Quenching

Take extreme caution when oil quenching. Flame-ups are very common and it's important to avoid wearing polyester and other meltable clothing.

Quenching is the process of heating up the edge of the blade and dunking it into mediums such as oil, water, polymer solutions, or brine. Quenching causes the formation of **martensite**, which is a hard and very brittle solution in iron and is the main constituent of hardened steel. Quenching causes soft, normalized steel to harden, becoming very brittle. In fact it will be brittle enough to just about shatter if you drop it. This level of hardness is too extreme for a usable blade, so after quenching it is important to ease off some of the hardness through a tempering process. Soft steel will easily bend and hardened steel will not. A sharpened edge on soft steel will dull out very quickly when used, so it's important to harden the blade.

Similar to normalizing, heat the blade to nonmagnetic and then just a little bit further to reach 1475°F–1500°F (801°C–815°C). When the blade reaches the desired heat, it should be quenched right away.

An old wives' tale says that you have to quench toward the north so that the earth's magnetic field doesn't pull your blade to the left or right. I won't call this nonsense, because I don't know if the knife gods are watching me write this, but to this day I quench to the north and haven't had many issues. . . .

When quenching a blade, you only really need to make sure that the cutting edge is hardened. This means the entire knife doesn't need to be dunked. As a beginner I didn't really understand this, but basically a soft blade is more flexible and less prone to snapping, so ideally you'll want to create a hard edge while leaving the spine of the blade soft. A great way to achieve this kind of hardness ratio is to do a differential quench. To obtain a proper differential heat treat, the edge needs to cool down faster than the spine. This leaves you with a softer spine and a harder edge. I hate seeing blades used to pry things open, but it's bound to happen and a soft spine will prevent the blade from snapping in the process.

Another method of differential heat treat is to use clay to insulate the spine so that it cools slower. This is a pretty effective method that I use quite a bit. You can use furnace cement, a mixture of clay, ashes, and salts, as well as high quality quenching clays.

You'll want to apply the clay while the blade is cool and make sure that it dries before quenching. I've also noticed that differential heat-treating can help prevent warping during the quench. And when using this method, it's common to notice a quench line or **hamon** that's created, showing the difference in hardness between the edge and the rest of the blade.

32 As you plunge your blade edge-first into the oil or medium of your choice, keep it moving forward and backward in a sort of cutting motion. Moving it side to side can lead to warps that are difficult to get out. Leave the blade in the quench container until the bubbling and smoking has stopped.

When quenching a blade, you only really need to make sure that the cutting edge is hardened. The entire knife doesn't need to be dunked.

33 If the blade warped at all during hardening, you have a short time period to straighten it out while it's still hot. You have to be very careful because the blade is brittle and very prone to breaking at this stage. I like to keep a slightly open vise near my quench tank that I can use to straighten out any warps. When your blade is quenched, it quickly cools off and regains its magnetism.

34 After quenching, you'll want to verify that the edge has been successfully hardened. Use a file to attempt cutting into the edge of the blade. If the file cuts in, then the blade is not hard. But if it skates off the edge, it's been successfully hardened. If the blade hasn't been hardened, it may be a case of decarburization, too low of a temperature before quench, or the wrong choice of steel.

Quenching Mediums

Blades are most commonly quenched in oil, but there are other mediums and the medium you use is completely up to you. Most oils benefit from being preheated to around 130F° (54°C) prior to quenching. This is because heating the oil lowers its viscosity, or thickness, and thinner oil cools faster.

You can preheat oil by using a burner or heating pad underneath the quenching vessel, or by first quenching scrap steel into the oil.

Canola oil makes for a great budget quenching oil and it's been a favorite of mine for a long time. Food-grade oils such as canola oil and **peanut oil** are both common choices for quenching. They also smell much better than some of the other oils when they heat up. Both canola oil and peanut oil should be preheated prior to use (see left).

Some knifemakers will use **motor oil,** new or used. An advantage is that this could potentially be a pretty cheap or free option, but motor oil comes with some disadvantages as well. Motor oil includes additives and potential toxins that are harmful when inhaled. Another downside to motor oils is that they smell really bad when used for quenching. They're also known to leave a black film on a blade that can be a hassle to remove.

Other quenching oils include **mineral oil** and **automatic transmission fluid**. These are potential alternatives to using motor oil. Mineral oil does not have the additives that are found in motor oil. **Baby oil** will also work, as it's similar to mineral oil, but it contains added perfumes.

And now we're on to the **commercial quenching oils**. There are many commercially available quenching oils on the market today. These commercial oils are designed specifically for quenching and are the ideal choice for many serious knifemakers. These oils can be very expensive and are often not available locally, however.

I very rarely quench in water or brine because they often cause blades to crack.

Alternative for Alloyed Steels: Air Hardening

Air hardening is another method of hardening a blade. With air hardening there is no quenching needed. The type of steel you are working with will determine whether or not your blade can be air hardened. One of the very first steels developed was just a plain carbon steel, and it has been the foundation of just about all other modern steels with the addition of different ingredients. Oil quenching steels have fewer alloys and primarily use only carbon to achieve their hardness. Air hardening steels have a higher quantity and/or percentage of alloys, on top of the carbon, such as vanadium, tungsten, and chromium. These alloys allow the steel to be hardened faster without a severe quench, but rather with the use of still or forced air.

Quench Safely

When quenching you need to be a safety nut. The container holding your quenching solution needs to be fireproof. I also recommend having a Class B fire extinguisher on standby. Oil likes to flame up when you quench hot steel into it. And if you knock over a

You will need a fireproof, watertight container for quenching.

bucket of flaming oil, fire will go everywhere that the oil goes. If I'm using a smaller quenching container, I'll surround it with a ring of bricks to prevent myself from kicking it over by mistake. I recommend keeping your quench container at least 10 ft. (3 m) from any combustible materials, and make sure you have a lid to smother flames if you need to. If you can do your quenching outside, that may be a safer option.

To avoid being burned yourself, it's wise to wear longer leather gloves and a welding style jacket. A face shield can protect against tall flames, but your best bet is to stand to the side when quenching.

Tempering

You can be an artist at the anvil and incredibly talented at the grinder, but until you understand the basics of heat-treating, aka tempering, your knives will be useless. When correctly performed, tempering will nicely balance the toughness and hardness of your blade.

Straight out of the quench, your blade is far too hard and brittle to serve as a functional tool. **Tempering** is the process of increasing the toughness of the steel by removing excess hardness. It involves heating the blade to a specific temperature below its critical heat for a specific period of time.

Tempering is a touchy subject and every knifemaker will pick up their own recipes and techniques as they gain experience. You can be surprisingly accurate with a household oven, but I'd recommend picking up an **infrared temperature gun** to verify that your oven is reading the proper heat.

You'll want to move onto tempering fairly quickly after the quench. I begin tempering my blades roughly fifteen minutes after they have been quenched, or once the blade has reached room temperature and is cool enough to touch. In its current state, your blade is prone to stress cracking due to its brittleness, so it is best to move onto the temper sooner than later.

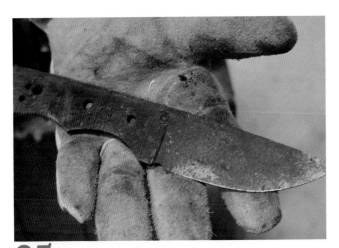

35 Clean up your blade with a wire brush and/or rag before putting it into an oven to avoid any dirt or oil burning up in the oven; this not only smells bad, it can also stain the blade.

36 Tempering requires the use of an oven. You can use a high quality kiln as well as a kitchen oven or even a toaster oven as a tempering vessel. Temper twice according to the chart.

OVEN TEMPERING

Tempering is generally done in two cycles. Oftentimes a blade will be put into the oven at a specific temperature for about one to two hours. The blade is then left out to cool completely, after which it is immediately placed back into the oven for a second cycle, usually at the same temperature and for the same duration. The temperature is based on the type of steel being tempered. The chart that I've created can be used as a guideline for tempering some of the more common knifemaking steels.

HEAT-TREATING GUIDE FOR COMMON STEELS						
TEMPER TWICE AT 2 HOURS PER CYCLE, ALLOWING THE STEEL TO COOL BETWEEN CYCLES						
STEEL TYPE	**APPROXIMATE HARDNESS AFTER QUENCH**	**400°F**	**450°F**	**500°F**	**550°F**	**600°F**
1080	65 RC	62-63 RC	61 RC	59-60 RC	58 RC	57 RC
1084	65 RC	62-63 RC	61 RC	59-60 RC	58 RC	57 RC
1095	66 RC	63 RC	61-62 RC	59-60 RC	57-58 RC	56-57 RC
O1	64 RC	59-60 RC	57-58 RC	56-57 RC	55-56 RC	54-55 RC
5160	63 RC	59 RC	58 RC	57 RC	55 RC	54 RC

When It Goes Wrong, Learn from Your Mistakes

These blades have both suffered from a poor heat treat. The dented and rolled-over edges tell me that the blades are too soft. These blades may have received tempering temperatures that were too high, resulting in a soft blade. Another cause to this problem may have been a failed quench that didn't truly harden the blades in the first place. This is why checking for hardness after the quench is very important.

A snapped tip lets me know that this blade might be too brittle and could have benefited from a higher tempering heat or additional normalizing cycle.

This box is what I call my "knife graveyard"; this is where many of my failed blades have ended up. Some of these have bad heat treats, warps, cracks or handle issues. Others I just happened to not like (I've become very critical of my work).

This is an example of failed epoxy. I found this blade in my "knife graveyard" and I believe the epoxy failed due to overheating the handle during shaping. See page 161 for more on this topic.

Tempering at a higher temperature will yield a softer material and a higher toughness, whereas lower tempering temperatures produce a harder and more brittle material. In other words, you may want to temper a survival knife at a higher temperature so that it will withstand more abuse without breaking, but if you want a knife that will hold an edge longer and require less sharpening you'll want to temper at a lower temperature. Finding a happy medium will result in a great heat treat.

Knife Use and Hardness

Keep in mind that the tempering temperature also depends on what the blade will be used for. For example, heavy-use blades require a softer temper. Hardness levels of steel are commonly measured on the Rockwell Scale in numbers given in RC units: the higher the number, the harder the steel.

Most axes, for example, have a lower hardness rating of around 50-54 RC so they can withstand the impacts involved in log and timberwork. Most pocketknives, on the other hand, have a hardness rating of around 58-60 RC since, because they aren't used for chopping or striking, they benefit from a harder edge.

Hardness scales can be both expensive and difficult to come across used. A great alternative to a scale is a set of hardness files. Hardness files generally come in sets of six files, each having a different hardness. You can use these to determine the hardness of your steel by checking to see which files bite into the steel and which ones don't, narrowing them down to a single file with a labeled hardness rating.

Practice makes perfect, and perfect is rare. If there is one thing I could go back and do as a beginner, it would be to spend more time learning tempering and the art of metallurgy. This is what makes or breaks a knife, literally speaking. To avoid faulty heat treats, practice and consistency are key.

Torch Tempering

If you don't have an oven, you can temper with the use of a torch. To temper with a torch you have to first clean off some of the forge and quench stains on the blade. This is because you'll need to be able to visualize the heat colors that the torch will be delivering to the blade.

While a torch temper works much faster than an oven temper, it's much harder to be consistent with your heat; an oven will almost always be more accurate. However, torch tempers are a nice option for small blades that will not encounter heavy-duty use, as well as for large blades or swords that won't fit into an oven.

Knife Hardness Scale

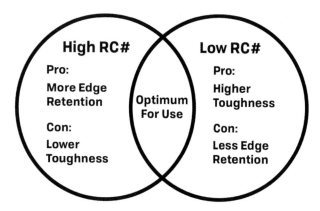

High RC#
Pro:
More Edge Retention
Con:
Lower Toughness

Optimum For Use

Low RC#
Pro:
Higher Toughness
Con:
Less Edge Retention

An advantage to tempering with a torch is that you're guaranteed to achieve a soft spine. Soft spines are good because they make for a much more flexible blade that is less prone to snapping.

To clean off the stain, use the same process that you did to grind the bevels. You don't need to create a perfect polish; going over the bevels with a 150-220 grit belt or medium-grit file will help to clean the surface just enough to easily judge the heat colors.

Secure the tang of the blade into a vice so that the edge is fully exposed. Use a fine torch nozzle no wider than ¾ in. (19 mm). Start by heating the spine of the blade, keeping the nozzle 2-3 in. (51–76 mm) away from the steel. Consistently move the torch back and forth along the spine and, as it heats up, you will begin to see color forming within the steel. Make sure to have a good light source because, when the blade begins to heat up, the colors will suddenly begin to show themselves and if you can't see it well you run the risk of overheating the edge.

It won't take long before your blade starts showing some color. The spine of the blade will become blue because it is the area where you're focusing the majority of the heat. The blue color will travel down toward the edge, in a sort of straw color. This straw color represents a successful tempering. Watch out:

It's very easy to mess up a torch temper. When you start to notice the spine turning blue, be very cautious because it is not long before that color extends toward the edge.

If you are torch tempering a double-sided blade, run the torch down the center of the blade and watch carefully as the colors extend to both edges. Again you're looking to achieve a pale yellowish, straw-colored cutting edge. Any darker will result in a blade that is too soft, and a lighter color will result in a blade that is too hard.

Alternative Tempering Methods

Tempering can also be done by leaving the blade to soak in a hot oil bath for extended periods of time, but this is more common in sword making, as larger blades would require a larger oven.

If you're using a coal or solid fuel forge, you can also temper a blade by resting the spine into the forge and watching as the colors travel up toward the edge.

A nice example of some colors that are encountered in the tempering process. Notice both the blue and the straw colors that are visible in the steel. Blue often means the tempering was done at too high a temperature, straw is just right.

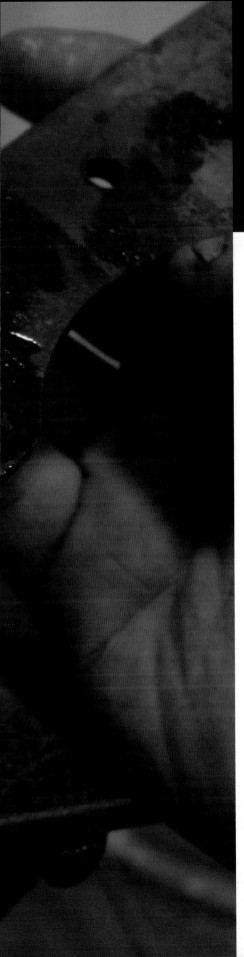

CHAPTER 6: FINISHING THE BLADE

Once you've achieved a normalized, quenched, and tempered blade, you'll probably notice that the bevels aren't as clean and shiny as they were when you first ground them. They've undoubtedly picked up quite a bit of forge and temper staining, caused by the heat and the oil or the quench medium. This is the part of the process where you will go back and clean up the bevels and make your knife blade shine again.

Cleaning Up the Forge Stains

If you remember from the initial grinding step (see page 88), the bevels have been left a little meatier than needed so as not to be too thin during the quench. This extra material also allows you some freedom to remove extra material while cleaning up the bevels now, after the quench.

Like I mentioned before, when you are initially grinding your bevels, you'll want to take them down to an edge thickness of about 0.010-0.025 in. (0.25–0.63 mm), depending on the style of knife. This creates a great starting position from which to begin creating the cutting edge. If your edge is still ⅛ in. (3 mm) thick, you'll want to take a step back and remove more material from your bevels until you have a thinner edge thickness. Remember that it's a good measure to leave about a 0.010–0.015 in. (0.25–0.38 mm) thickness at the end of the primary bevel on a standard outdoor knife before creating the cutting edge or "micro-bevel." A kitchen knife might be left with about a 0.005 in. (0.127 mm) edge thickness and a heavier-use knife might be left with closer to a 0.025 in. (0.63 mm) edge thickness.

PICK UP WHERE YOU LEFT OFF

When cleaning up bevels, you'll want to take your knife back to the belt grinder (or your abrasive tool of choice) and begin to remove the forge stains, using the same grit that you left off with before. If you brought the blade up to 120 grit before quench, start cleaning the bevels to get a clean 120 grit finish again. Unless you've left a lot of extra material to take off, you're not trying to hog off a lot of material in this step.

Cooling the steel is a constant duty throughout this process.

KEEP IT COOL

It is quite possible to ruin the heat treat now that this blade has been tempered, so you need to be *very careful* not to overheat the steel from here on out. Taking the steel past its tempering temperature will result in ruining your current hardness. My advice is to play it safe by dunking your steel into water anytime it starts to get hot. Using higher grit belts will cause the steel to heat up faster, so cooling the steel will be a constant duty throughout this process.

I never wear gloves while post-temper grinding; this way I can immediately feel if the blade is getting too hot. If you are using files or other hand tools you're probably in the clear, but if you take the blade to a grinder again just remember to keep it cool.

Satin or Hand-Sanded Finish

There are many ways to go about finishing a blade and it often comes down to personal preference. For example, you can just sharpen the edge and call it quits, but you can also clean off the forge stain and go as far as to give it a hand-sanded satin finish or even a mirror polish. A polished edge is a more corrosion-resistant edge because it contains very little pitting or creasing where moisture can be trapped.

Creating a satin or hand-sanded finish is my personal favorite method of bevel finishing. After I clean up my bevels in post temper, using about a 120 grit belt, I'll then move up in belt grits, removing the grind lines from the previous grit and switching belts each time I create a new uniform finish. My belt progression is as follows: 120, 220, 320, 400, 600. When post-temper grinding I use ceramic or alumina zirconia belts. Higher quality surface conditioning belts are also available and often come in the form of a Scotch-Brite-like material attached to a belt.

After the blade has been brought up to a uniform

400–600 grit, I'll start to hand-sand. When hand-sanding, you're changing the direction of the abrasive to create a grain that follows the length of the bevel rather than going perpendicular against it. Use a wet/dry style of sandpaper. A drop of cutting oil can be helpful during this process, as it can help prevent the sandpaper from gathering dust.

37 For this task, the blade is clamped into place face up so that one side can be worked at a time.

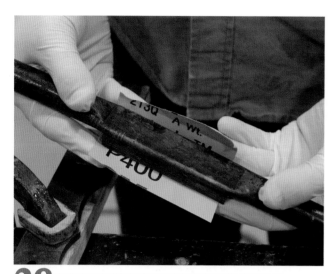

38 The use of a sanding stick can be a great way to sand bevels. A sanding stick can be wood, metal, or plastic and often only an inch (25 mm) in width and about a foot (30 cm) in length. This can be used as a tool by attaching sandpaper to the center, then gripping the outsides and using them as handles. I recommend starting with a paper at least one grit size under the grit that you've finished at the belt grinder with. For example, if you take the bevels up to 600 grit on the belt sander, start hand-sanding at around 400 grit.

39 The sandpaper needs to be pulled back and forth across the length of the bevel using light pressure. If your sanding stick has sharp corners, wrap them with the sandpaper to help reach tight areas such as the plunge lines. You're not only polishing the blade, but you're also changing the grain direction, and using a lower grit can help to obtain the proper grain direction faster. When hand-sanding, the lower level of the grits should generally consume the longest amount of time. Hand-sand until all signs of the previous grind lines have been removed. Circular hand-sanding motions can help out during the lower grits, but always finish with a series of smooth pulls down the entire length of the bevel—this will result in the smoothest finish.

40 Once you've achieved a clean and even-looking finish using the lower grit, move back up to about 600 grit. This time there are no perpendicular grind lines to remove, so you'll only need to focus on front-to-back pushing and pulling down the length of the bevel. Continue until you've created a smooth 600 grit finish. Oftentimes this is where I'll stop when creating a hand-sanded finish, but experiment with the different grits and find out which fits your style the best. Hand-sanded finishes typically range from 400 grit to 1000 grit, and it all comes down to personal preference. If you notice any imperfections or out-of-line sanding marks, go back and rework the areas. Hand-sanding takes a lot of patience, and I don't often see beginners taking the time to do it.

Mirror Polish

To create a mirror finish, follow the same initial steps as you would to create a satin finish. Once you're ready to hand-sand, use circular motions between each grit. Constantly change the direction of your sanding, so as to not establish a direction of grind line. To achieve a mirror finish, much higher grits of sandpaper must be used. My sandpaper progress for a mirror finish is 400, 600, 800, 1000, 1500, 2000, and sometimes I'll go as far as 3000 grit.

Buffing the Blade

Buffing wheels can be used to improve the polish on a blade. This is an optional step that can also be a substitute for polishing on a grinder or hand-sanding.

Soft cotton cloth buffing wheels. These are available at any big-box hardware store.

1. First of all, it's important to have a different wheel dedicated to each compound you use. Otherwise they will get mixed up and won't work the way they are meant to.

2. It's also important to always run a wheel in the same direction. Over time, a wheel forms to the direction it's being used in. Running the wheel in reverse can cause a poorer finish, and your workpiece can be more easily grabbed and thrown by the wheel. Which brings me to my next point.

3. Buffing wheels can be very dangerous. It's important to use a firm grip on your workpiece and never force it into the wheel. Always allow the tool to do the work, take your time, and the results will come.

Many buffers are variable-speed machines. Knifemakers often run these machines at about 1800 rpm or 3600 rpm. I always recommend running a buffer at around **1800 rpm** because it's safer for most operations. Taking your time with steps

such as buffing a knife bevel is important because if you remove too much material, it can't exactly be put back on the blade, and you may have to start over. Patience is a must in creating a beautiful finished product.

WHEELS

There are a few common types of wheels and compounds that you'll encounter when buffing a blade. The first wheel is known as a **felt wheel.** These are available in multiple densities varying from soft to hard. Soft wheels are great to use on rounded surfaces and tasks requiring less pressure. Harder wheels are commonly used on flat surfaces and when heavier pressure is necessary.

Another common wheel is known as a **muslin buff**. Muslin buffs are made from high grade processed cotton. These are very versatile wheels and are a popular choice for general-purpose use. A sewn muslin wheel can be used with almost any compound, making them extremely versatile. A loose muslin wheel is often used for final finishing and cleanup work. A polishing muslin wheel is a very hard sewed and glued wheel with a canvas cover on either side to generate added strength. Polishing wheels are most often used with greaseless compounds as well as cut-and-color bars, which I go over shortly.

Patience is a must in creating a beautiful finished product.

Another common style of buffing wheel is known as a **sisal wheel**. Sisal wheels are special wheels used with cut-and-color bars. They are not to be used with greases compounds or rouges, as these wheels will not hold onto compounds other than cut-and-color bars.

COMPOUNDS

Like buffing wheels, there are many different compounds to choose from. Greaseless compounds are perhaps one of the more popular compounds to encounter in knifemaking. There are two styles of greaseless compounds; **plasticlad solid** and **brush-on paste**. Both of these styles are glue-based and are most commonly used on muslin or felt wheels. Plasticlad solid is available in a multitude of grits ranging from 80 grit, which is the coarsest grit, to 600 grit, the finest. The available grits are commonly used sequentially to polish a piece of material.

Brush-on compound offers grits ranging from 150 to 800. The brush-on compound lasts up to four to five times longer that the plasticlad once it has been set up on the wheel, but the downside is that it must be left to dry for at least three to four hours after it's been applied in order to be used properly.

Cut-and-color bars are an example of a grease-based compound. This is a buffing compound most often available in medium and finer grits that's used to remove scratches left behind by greaseless compounds. They are available in medium to finer grades and are generally used to achieve a satin finish when applied to a sisal wheel.

White rouge is another style of grease-based compound, used to create a bright mirror finish. White rouge is the most popular of all the buffing compounds. It can be used on a wide range of materials, such as steel, plastic, brass, and fiberglass.

Black emery is a course compound used for cutting or preparing materials to be buffed. **Red rouge** is used for soft or finer metals and can bring them up to a mirror finish. **White diamond** is courser than red rouge and is used for removing deeper scratches from metals.

To remove heavier material such as rust, scale, or pits, apply 80 to 150 grit greaseless compound to a felt or polishing muslin wheel. If you've already cleaned up the blade at the belt grinder, these lower grits can be skipped over.

To start polishing your blade, begin with about a 200 grit greaseless compound applied to a sewn muslin wheel. Continue to work out any scratches from the previous abrasive. Then, using the same technique, move up in greaseless compound grits from 300 to 400 and finally 600.

To create a dull satin finish, you'll need to use a cut-and-color bar compound. Apply the cut-and-color bar compound to a sisal wheel to blend the scratches from the previous greaseless compound. A white rouge compound on a loose muslin wheel is commonly used when creating a mirror finish.

Creating the Cutting Edge

41 Now that your primary bevels are cleaned up and looking good, it's time to create a micro bevel. A micro bevel is a secondary bevel at the bottom of your primary bevel that actually creates the sharp cutting edge. Keep in mind that a primary bevel CAN be ground down to a thin enough edge to be sharp on its own, but this will result in a much weaker edge that is too thin for any heavy use. Adding a micro bevel strengthens the edge of the blade. It is created with an angle that is a few degrees wider than the angle of the primary bevel.

42 To create a micro bevel, you can use the same tools as you did to create the primary bevel. Whether you are using a belt grinder or a hand file, just adjust to a slightly wider angle than you did before. Try to do full sweeps down the entirety of the edge rather than start and stop a few times to create a full pass. This will keep you more consistent and help to build muscle memory with the tool. Always use light pressure to avoid removing more material than desired.

Keep Micro Bevels Consistent

To keep your micro bevel consistent on either side, you can scribe a line down the center of the edge, as I recommended doing during the primary beveling process (see page 86). Scribing a line can be done with a drill bit of the same thickness as the blade steel, or by using a height gauge. The scribed line can be used as a reference for grinding. Carefully grind the first side of the micro bevel up to the line, and then the other side. I recommend starting with a medium-grit abrasive or file to start things off, and as you get close to the scribe line, switching over to a medium-high grit.

Sharpening the Blade Using a Whetstone

Sharpening is what makes or breaks a knife. Basically, a dull knife is just plain embarrassing. If a knife doesn't cut, it doesn't work.

As a beginner I found sharpening to be a painstaking process. I learned that one of the keys to achieving a sharp blade is to create a good edge profile during beveling. If your bevel design is too steep or too shallow, you'll find it to be more difficult to properly sharpen the knife's edge. So when grinding your bevels, do yourself a favor and be sure to consider the sharpening process down the road.

First, take those lousy pull-through sharpeners and throw them in the garbage. Those things are never going to match your bevel perfectly and you'll constantly be re-profiling your grind without even realizing it. They'll also scratch and dirty-up any nicely polished bevel. Before I go in depth about sharpening, I'll start by saying that everyone has his or her own techniques and preferences. As you start practicing, you'll find out what methods work best for you.

The most common and, in my opinion, most effective way to sharpen a blade is with the use of whetstones. A **whetstone** is a fine-grained stone used for sharpening a variety of tools. Many whetstones are two-sided and feature both a higher grit and a lower grit. Two-sided whetstones are available in a multitude of grits, but what I'd recommend to anyone is the very common 400/1000 grit stone. Learning to properly use a whetstone takes some practice and requires you to build up some muscle memory, but once you have the process down, you'll be unstoppable. I remember my first whetstone. I must have sharpened every knife in my mom's kitchen.

Keep It Dry

The most common mistake when using a whetstone is to get it wet. Contrary to popular belief, "whet" does not mean "wet"; it means to sharpen with grinding or friction. Many people have dowsed their whetstones with water or oil, and all this does is trap small metal particles within the liquid, which in turn makes for a rougher edge. Now, there is a Japanese stone referred to as a "waterstone." A waterstone is a real, natural stone, and when water is added it causes the stone's surface to dissolve, creating a gritty mud that acts as an abrasive for sharpening.

How to Use a Whetstone

To use a whetstone, first start by placing the stone on a strong work surface such as a cutting board or workbench. I recommend placing a towel or a non-slip mat underneath the stone to prevent it from sliding.

With the coarser side of the stone facing up, firmly grasp the handle of the knife and place the edge against the stone.

A dull knife is just plain embarrassing.

Make sure the entire edge makes contact with the stone, then, using a sweeping movement, glide the micro bevel across the stone. Keep the blade at an angle of about 22°. This angle will vary slightly based on the profile of your bevel. Use your secondary hand to stabilize and apply minimal pressure to the blade. I prefer to keep the edge pointed away from me the entire time.

Make ten passes before switching to the other side of the blade. After about ten to twenty passes on either side, you should begin to notice a very fine burr beginning to develop on the edge. This is a good indication that it's time to flip the stone over and begin using the finer grit.

Make ten to fifteen passes on either side of the blade using the higher grit. It's good practice to finish things off by doing one or two passes on either side of the blade to push that burr back and forth until it ultimately falls off. If the burr continues to hang on, don't worry: you can remove it during the honing process that comes next.

Allow about ten passes on the stone and then flip the blade over and repeat this on the other side. Continue the process until you've created a razor-sharp edge. Many people will test edge sharpness by trying to shave the hair from an arm or leg, this may be a great way to display sharpness but it can be dangerous as well. I prefer to visually inspect the edge. Using my fingers, I slowly and carefully feel the edge for any irregularities that indicate a dull edge.

From left: leather strop, diamond rod, ceramic rod, whetstone.

Honing the Blade

Congratulations! At this point you've created a razor-sharp blade. Now let's make it a little bit sharper still by honing it.

Honing is a way to sharpen a blade without removing or grinding away any material. Honing is used to do touch-ups during field use, remove burrs, or to complete the sharpening process after whetstone sharpening. Honing is most commonly done using a ceramic rod (commonly found in a kitchen) or a leather strop. A blade that is consistently honed after use will very rarely require any heavy sharpening.

LEATHER STROPS

My favorite way to hone a blade is with the use of a leather strop. This can be done either after a ceramic rod or instead of a ceramic rod. If you've ever been to a classic barbershop for a straight razor shave, you may have seen the barber start by flicking the blade back and forth across a strip of leather. This is an example of stropping.

A strop is basically just a piece of leather. There have been plenty of times that I've been out camping and used my belt to strop my knife, and it works great. You'll want to use the rough side of the leather, and by adding buffing compound you can even use the strop to help polish the edge of the blade in the process. There are many specialty honing and stropping compounds on the market today, and they all work great for this process. You can also buy ready-made strops.

Some leather strops are mounted onto blocks while others are loose like a belt. I haven't noticed a difference in effectiveness between the two styles, but I personally find the loose belt-style strops easier to use. I have a leather strop hanging on a wall in my shop. This allows me to walk over, pull out the bottom to create tension, and strop the blade on the taut leather.

When using a block-mounted strop, you'll want to be sure to keep it secure when in use. Stropping

43 Apply buffing compound to a leather strop. This helps polish the edge of the blade.

44 Keep tension on the strop while stropping. With the edge of the blade down on the strop, draw the blade back toward you. Make one pass, then do the same on the other side.

requires you to use some pressure, and the nice thing about the belt-style strop is that the hand holding the leather taut is far away from the moving blade. When using a block-mounted strop, you need to hold it in place, meaning your hand is near the moving blade. A way to avoid this is to secure your block with a clamp or vise.

Firmly grasp your knife with the blade facing away from you. To properly use a strop, reach out and place the edge down on the strop. Use light pressure and draw the blade back toward you, keeping a slightly wider angle than you did during initial sharpening. Start near the ricasso and pull the tip toward the strop as you draw the blade. This technique allows you to strop the full length of the blade in a single pass.

After a single pass, flip the blade over and do the same to the other side. If it makes things easier, you can allow the blade to face you, and by gripping the handle in reverse you can push the blade away and up the strop. Your method will come down to personal preference as you get better. The most important thing to remember is to keep a tight grip on the knife and stay safe.

From my experience, stropping is the absolute best way to remove burrs left over from sharpening. It also helps to align the cutting edge, as well as polish and smooth out the blade. I'll skip over the ceramic rod from time to time, but I never forget to strop a knife. Stropping is such an easy and effective way to maintain an edge over time. I recommend keeping a small strop in any camping bag or toolbox—keeping up with honing prevents you from having to do heavy sharpening.

> *I never forget to strop a knife.*

Check Sharpness with a Cheap Pen

Another great option is to use the "pen check." To do this, you just need a cheap, soft, plastic pen. Hold the pen against a sturdy surface, and with your other hand, rest the blade against the pen as you would on a whetstone. Gently push the blade forward, allowing the edge to tilt slightly into the pen, as if you were carving with absolutely no effort or pressure at all. If the blade bites into the plastic, you know that you have a sharp edge. If it skates across without cutting or biting in, take a step back and spend a few more minutes at the whetstone.

CERAMIC RODS

Honing a blade with a ceramic rod is a very simple process. You've probably seen chefs sharpening their kitchen knives this way. Steel rods and diamond rods are also available, but ceramic rods are more forgiving and, in my opinion, a better option for knife honing.

Generally speaking, any form of honing should be done at a slightly wider angle than the sharpening. You're putting the attention more directly onto the very edge, or where a burr may be found. Gripping the knife handle firmly in one hand and the ceramic rod in the other, begin to glide the knife down the length of the rod, starting near the ricasso and pulling the tip toward the rod as you go. This technique will allow you to make contact with the full length of the blade in a single pass. After one pass, do the same on the other side of the blade. Make sure to use very light pressure and keep your angle slightly wider than you did during initial sharpening. Often only three passes on either side will be sufficient in removing any possible burrs and leaving a hair-popping edge on the blade.

Honing with a ceramic rod is similar to sharpening with a whetstone, in that it takes some practice to get good at. When I first started using a ceramic rod, I got pretty good with one side of the blade, and when I flipped it over to repeat the process it felt awkward, as if I were writing with my non-dominant hand. So keep in mind that you'll build up some muscle memory over time, and the process will only get easier.

Please don't use your ceramic rod at light-speed like you see master chefs doing; you're just asking to get injured. And rushing a process like this could cause imperfections in your edge, forcing you to start over.

Using a ceramic rod to hone the blade's edge.

CHAPTER 7: CHOOSING HANDLE MATERIAL

After you have finished creating the blade of the knife, you'll want to make the handle. While a blade can still serve its purpose without a handle, securing a nice handle to the blade is what makes it comfortable to use. When I'm selling my knives at a knife show, customers don't get the chance to take the knives out for a test drive like they would with a car. The buyer really only gets to hold the knife in his or her hand to see how it feels. Because of this fact, I look at the handle as a big selling point, but even if it's for a knife that I'm not selling, I still want the best handle I can make, for myself.

There are a ridiculous number of handle material options available. Prior to selecting handle material, you will want to consider what types of tasks and environments the knife will encounter.

Leather-stacked handle featuring G10 spacers, a brass bolster, and buttcap. You see cordage wrap on a lot of survival knife handles because the cordage can be removed and used elsewhere if needed.

Natural handle materials such as **wood** or **antler** offer a very traditional look. They can be quite beautiful and, generally speaking, they hold up pretty well. The drawback to natural materials is that they have a tendency to expand and contract over time according to changes in humidity and temperature. Some **synthetic varieties** of handle material offer extreme durability, strength, and resistance to weather. Wood, antler, and synthetic materials are all very common handle material options and especially good for beginners.

I'd recommend that beginners stay away from materials like **mammoth ivory, mother of pearl, gold,** or even some **resin casts**. Not only are these materials expensive, they can also be difficult to work with.

You can get incredible results with some of the more expensive materials, but looking back at some of my earlier knives, I wish I'd have saved that superior material for the more seasoned skill set that I have today. Materials are completely up to you as the creator; just keep in mind that it's not a bad idea to start off with more affordable materials as a beginner. Expensive materials don't make for an expensive knife, the value is in the skill level of its maker. A master bladesmith might spend $20 on material and create a blade that far surpasses the quality of an intermediate knife maker that spends $100 on material.

Handles are Practical, Too

A good handle can prevent injury caused by dropping the knife or by the hand slipping up onto the blade. It also prevents hand fatigue caused by an uncomfortable grip.

Sourcing Handle Material

If you're buying handle material from a knifemaking supplier, you'll notice that the handle material is sold either in a block or as scales. A **block** is an individual piece of handle material commonly used for hidden-tang knives. It's often drilled or burned to receive a tang. So rather than attach handle material to either side of a tang, you put the hidden tang through the center of the handle material. Because of this you only need one piece of material to create a hidden-tang handle. Blocks come in a variety of sizes, but most are around 1½ × 2 × 5 in. (38 × 51 × 127 mm).

Scales are a pair of book-matched handle pieces used for full-tang knife handles. They are basically made from a block that has been split down the middle. Each of the two handle pieces is half the thickness of a block and designed to be placed on either side of a tang. You can either purchase a set of scales or cut a block down the center to create a set yourself.

If you are buying odd-sized material, large pieces of lumber, or even sourcing your own wood from your yard or a forest, you'll want to square them up accordingly to fit the size of your handle. Sometimes local forests will be able to provide good quality pieces of wood that can be used for handle material, but always check for permission before harvesting wood locally.

Scales are often no thicker than ½ in. (13 mm) per scale. If your material is too thick to begin with or if you're splitting a block down the middle, use a band saw to do the job. A band saw will give you the cleanest cut, and the kerf of the blade is so very thin that you won't lose much material in the process. You can also use a table saw or a handheld rip saw; just make sure that the blade is compatible with the material you're cutting.

Desert ironwood handle for a Damascus knife.

WOOD

When selecting wood to use as a handle material, understand that wood will need to be either stabilized or well oiled to prevent the elements from penetrating its pores. **Stabilizing** is a common practice that involves placing dry wood along with a stabilizing solution into a sealed container and then using a vacuum and high pressure to impregnate the wood with the stabilizing solution. Stabilizing fills any voids in the wood with a resin-like solution, making the wood stronger. Properly stabilized wood is more durable and less likely to develop issues in the future. Some species of wood such as **desert ironwood** or **African blackwood**, which are a couple favorites of mine, are very oily woods and are naturally stable and solid. Other species of wood benefit greatly from being stabilized.

A look at the front of a pair of book-matched knife scales.

A simple version of the stabilization process is to just leave the handle material to soak in oil (boiled linseed oil works well) overnight. This can be done after the wood has been attached to the tang of the blade. Oftentimes, after I've shaped and attached a wooden handle, I'll leave the handle of the knife to soak for at least eight hours in boiled linseed oil. Pre-stabilized wood can be purchased from most knifemaking suppliers, but they're often about $10 more expensive than un-stabilized wood.

Many woods benefit from being **book-matched** against each other. When wood is ripped down the middle and the two pieces are folded outward, the wood grain can align with the neighboring piece quite nicely, creating a book match. These pieces can then be stacked with their grain in alignment to create a nice flowing grain pattern in the finished handle.

JANKA SCALE

Similar to steel, there is a hardness scale for different species of wood. On the Janka Wood Hardness Scale, the higher the number, the harder the wood. **Ebony** for example is a very hard wood with a Janka rating of 3220, and **poplar** is a much softer wood with a Janka rating of 540. A harder wood ultimately means less denting or marring during use. Softer woods such as **mahogany** or **yellow pine** might look nice but they are much more prone to being damaged during use. I avoid using woods with a Janka rating of less than 1000. **Oak, maple,** and **walnut** are a few great examples of handle material that can be found at many of the big box hardware stores, but if you'd like something with more pattern and character, you might try searching for an exotic species of wood such as **Honduras rosewood** or **tigerwood**.

> *I tend to avoid using woods with a Janka rating of less than 1000.*

You'll notice pretty quickly that there's an almost endless list of wood species, and it'll take you a lifetime to experiment with each one. I strongly recommend starting with a cheaper and simpler hardwood such as **oak, maple, hickory,** or **walnut**. Each of these woods work great for a knife handle, and their price tags won't break your heart if you make a mistake.

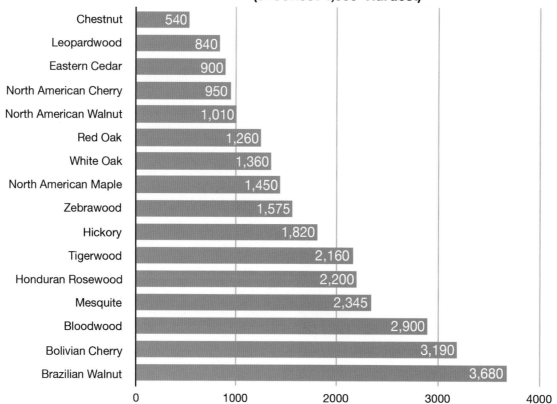

Wood hardness ratings according to the Janka Scale:
(0=Softest 4,000=Hardest)

Chestnut	540
Leopardwood	840
Eastern Cedar	900
North American Cherry	950
North American Walnut	1,010
Red Oak	1,260
White Oak	1,360
North American Maple	1,450
Zebrawood	1,575
Hickory	1,820
Tigerwood	2,160
Honduran Rosewood	2,200
Mesquite	2,345
Bloodwood	2,900
Bolivian Cherry	3,190
Brazilian Walnut	3,680

Synthetic Material

The synthetic handle material category offers a wide variety of man-made materials, some of which are perhaps the strongest and most durable options available on the market. The huge advantage to a synthetic material over wood is that it is far more weather resistant. Synthetic materials may include fiberglass laminates, high-density plastics, resin casts, or even carbon fiber.

Micarta, also known as phenolic laminate, is perhaps the most popular form of synthetic handle material and is sought after for its strength and durability. Micarta is a trademark and specific product from Norplex-Micarta. The term Micarta is often used incorrectly as a common title for what should be referred to as phenolic laminate. Phenolic laminate is a laminated plastic created by layering materials such as canvas, linen, or paper. The layered materials are impregnated with a resin and then formed using heat and pressure. Phenolic laminate often provides more grip than other synthetic materials, and it takes a little more patience to achieve a high shine or polish.

G10 is another very popular choice of synthetic handle material among knifemakers. It is a glass-based pressure laminate. It is quite similar to phenolic laminate in both application and looks. G10 often provides a smoother overall finish compared to phenolic laminate. This material is favored for its strength and resistance to moisture. It was first used as a substrate for printed circuit boards, so G10 naturally has a high level of electrical insulation and chemical resistance, if that means anything to you.

Carbon fiber is a strong yet very lightweight material. It's simply a carbon fiber laminate formed by compressing layers of material soaked in phenolic resin, very similar to Micarta and G10.

A couple of identical blade designs featuring black G10 and jade ghost G10 handle material.

Phenolic laminate handle.

Pins

Handle pins are commonly found in the majority of full-tang knives, as well as many hidden-tang knives. A pin is a piece of hardware that adds strength by physically connecting a tang to its handle material. Similar to steel or handle material, pins are available in a wide range of styles and materials. A very simple version of a handle pin is nothing more than a piece of steel or brass rod that is cut to size and glued into a pinhole (I'll discuss pinholes more in the next section). More advanced styles of pins will include threaded studs or bolts for added strength and clamping pressure.

A pin not only adds strength to a knife, it can also provide some flare to a handle. Larger pins might stand out a bit more than smaller pins, and brass pins might look nicer than steel pins against certain woods. Metal pins will often provide more strength than synthetic pins, but they will also weigh more and have the potential to rust or patina. Keep these things in mind when selecting your pins.

A combat style knife featuring both steel and carbon fiber handle pins.

Solid Rods

Rods can be found at most hardware stores or steel suppliers. (The term **rod** refers to a long piece of material that **pins** are cut from.) Brass and steel rods are very commonly used by many knifemakers. Rods can also be made from G10, carbon fiber, Micarta, and many other synthetic materials. These many options allow you to achieve different colors and textures.

Rods come in a variety of thicknesses and it's up to you what size you want to use. A few common thicknesses are ⅛, ³⁄₁₆, and ¼ in. (3, 5, and 6 mm). When mounted into a vise, metal rods can be cut easily with a hacksaw. Angle grinders and band saws will also do the trick. The length of your pins should be a hair longer than the thickness of your block (hidden-tang handle), or the thickness of both scales combined with the tang (full-tang handle).

Allowing a little bit of excess length is a good idea because, in order to easily place the pins into the pinholes, you'll need to chamfer the ends. Chamfering the ends removes any burrs that were left over from cutting and allows the pin to enter the hole much easier. If the ends are chamfered, you'll have gaps in the pinholes surrounding the chamfered ends. I cut my pins just long enough to allow the chamfered ends to protrude from either side.

Rod-style pins are perhaps the easiest type of handle hardware to install. Unlike other types of pins, there are no threaded studs or bolts to be recessed into the handle.

Brass, steel, and aluminum rods.

A hollow rod is used to create the option for an added lanyard toward the back of the handle.

HOLLOW RODS FOR LANYARD USE

Hollow rods, or tubing, are commonly used to create a lanyard hole. Many heavy-use knives will incorporate a lanyard hole toward the back of the handle. This allows the user to connect his or her hand to the handle using a piece of cordage. A hollow rod can be used in place of a solid rod to easily create a lanyard hole.

Hollow rods can be found at local hardware stores, and, like solid rods, they come in a variety of material types and thicknesses. When selecting a hollow rod, keep in mind the thickness of the rope or cordage that you'd like to use as a lanyard because it will need to fit within the hole created by the tube. It's common to use paracord as a lanyard material because of its strength and the wide variety of colors in which it is available. Paracord can be found at many big box hardware or sporting goods stores.

Lanyard Pros and Cons

Many knife users and makers are big fans of lanyards. It's a great way to store some extra rope, and provide some extra security when using a knife. However, I'm very cautious about using lanyards and I'll tell you why: When your knife is in its sheath, the end of the handle and the lanyard are exposed. This means that if you're hiking through thick brush, for example, it's very easy for a bush or a tree branch to steal your knife from you as you hike by. Now imagine you're doing the same thing, just hiking by, and your knife is in your hand with the lanyard unconnected. If the lanyard were to catch a bush or a branch, the knife could be pulled through the back of your hand, allowing the blade to pass over all of your fingers. When I use a lanyard, I prefer to connect one as needed, rather than let it hang loose when it's not in use.

Mosaic Rods

Mosaic rods are an excellent way to add flare to a knife handle. A mosaic rod is essentially made by inserting many small rods into a hollow rod. The small rods are often arranged to create a pattern and the voids are then filled with epoxy. The epoxy is sometimes dyed to add color to the patterning. Mosaic rods are quite a bit pricier than your standard rod, and are often only available through knifemaking suppliers.

Clamping Bolts

Any handle fastener that features a threaded stud or a bolt will provide more strength than your standard rod. With the addition of a threaded bolt, clamping pressure will be provided to your handle material, preventing full-tang scales from ever popping loose should the epoxy happen to fail. The clamping pressure will also help during the glue-up stage of your handle material, which we'll discuss in the next section. Below are a couple common styles of clamping bolts that can be used in a knife handle.

LOVELESS BOLTS

The loveless bolt is sold as a screw or stud with a nut for either side. To use a loveless bolt, the two nuts must be partially recessed or countersunk into either side of the handle material and in line with a pinhole drilled to fit the stud. With the nuts in place, tightening the screw will draw the scales together against the tang, creating a clamping pressure. When the excess pin material is later ground off, a sort of bird's eye effect is created. This effect can be enhanced for example by using brass nuts and a stainless steel stud.

CORBY BOLTS

Corby bolts are similar to loveless bolts in that they need to be countersunk into the handle material. The difference is that Corby bolts are made of only two parts, a male and a female bolt, which are screwed together. The heads of the Corby bolts must be countersunk into the handle material while the threads meet in between the tang. Tightening these bolts creates a clamping pressure and helps to provide a very secure handle.

A Corby bolt (left) and a Loveless bolt, both unassembled.

A Corby bolt (left) and a Loveless bolt, both assembled.

CHAPTER 8: ATTACHING A HANDLE

After you've selected the handle material that best fits your style, it's time to attach it to the tang. Attaching a handle is not always an easy task, especially for a beginner. There are a lot of important little steps that make up that portion of the knifemaking process. I've failed here more than anywhere else, so I recommend taking your time and planning things out to guarantee your success in this chapter

Really take your time during the handle preparation process because this is oftentimes the step that leads to the most mistakes for beginning knifemakers.

Making a Full-Tang Knife Handle

When making a full-tang knife handle, you'll be working with scales, which are two separate pieces that are to be attached to either side of the tang (see my earlier description on page 128). If you're starting with one thicker block of material, it will have to be ripped down the middle to create two scales. If you're starting out with a thinner strip of material, it will have to be chopped up to create two scales. Unless you're beginning with pre-made scales, odds are you will have to make some cuts to get your handle material down to a workable size. A thickness of about ¼ to ⅜ in. (6–10 mm) is generally a good starting point for each scale, depending on the size of your knife.

A band saw is a very popular choice among knifemakers for ripping, cross cutting, and shaping handle material. A quality band saw can be quite the investment and well worth it, but it's not critical to create a spectacular handle.

45 Use a band saw (or handsaw) to cut scales. A handsaw is a great addition to a knife shop, as it's great for processing smaller pieces of handle material. Whether you're using wood, bone, high density plastic, or metal, it's important to make sure to use the proper blade to cut the material you're working with.

46 Once your material has been cut and processed down to scales of a workable size, you'll want to make sure that they are nice and flat. Most knifemakers will flatten handle material against the platen (flat metal surface behind the belt) on a belt grinder. Flattening by hand is as easy as placing sandpaper onto a flat surface such as a piece of glass and continuously pulling your handle material over the top of it.

47 Check for flatness by holding the scales against a flat surface such as a ruler or a square and then check the edges for gaps. Mark any high spots with a pencil and continue to flatten the surface until there are no longer any gaps. Once you've flattened both scales, check them once more against each other to verify they are sitting nicely.

Attaching Liners

If you plan to attach liners to your handle scales, now is a great time to do so. Most liner material will come in large sheets, or scale-sized pieces. The material I'm working with in this example is black G10 liner material. This liner material has been cut from a larger sheet to fit the scales appropriately. To cut this material, I use a band saw. A razor blade may also do the trick.

In order to ensure a successful glue-up, I've roughed up the faces of the liners to ensure that it has some tooth or grip for the epoxy to cling onto. After mixing up a 2-step epoxy made up from a resin and hardener, I evenly spread the solution onto the liners. Then, using some light clamping pressure, I attach the scales to the glued surfaces of the liners and let them be while the epoxy cures. I'll go more in depth with the epoxy process when we get into the handle-attaching section (see page 154).

Liners are a great way to add some flair to a full tang handle. Liners are thin pieces of material that are used as spacers between a knife tang and the handle scales. These are most often made from a synthetic material such as vulcanized fiber or G10. If your handle scales are too thin to begin with, liners can be used to add some width to the handle material.

Preparing Handle Pins

Now that your handle material has been processed and flattened, pins must be used to secure it to the tang. There are many different types of pins, as discussed in the last chapter, and it's completely up to you which ones you use. I'll be going over the most common method of pinning, which is to use solid rods.

Solid rods are most often cut from a larger piece of stock. Whether you are using metal or synthetic rods, you'll want to make sure to use the proper tools to cut them. You'll also want to match the size of your handle pins to the size of the holes that have been drilled into your blade's tang.

48 Clamping the rod in a vise is a great way to keep it secure during cutting. Metal rods are best cut using a hacksaw or an angle grinder equipped with a cutoff wheel. Most synthetic rods can be cut at the band saw or with a handsaw using the proper blade.

49 Holes will be drilled into the handle material in alignment with the holes in the tang, but prior to drilling into the handle material the pins must be cut, because they will serve as locator pins to keep the holes in alignment. Once the pins are cut to size, lightly chamfer the ends to improve ease of entry into the drilled holes. Chamfering pins is most commonly done at the belt grinder but can also be done using a hand file.

DRILLING PINHOLES

With the pins prepared, it's just about time to drill holes into the handle material. Start by stacking the scales and lightly wrapping the ends with masking tape to help keep them together. Once secured, overlay the material with the tang of the knife to verify that it fits within the handle material you've selected and cut out. It's at this point that I like to trace the perimeter of the handle with a marker to create a guideline that can be referenced later.

Make sure you have a clean and flat surface to drill on, otherwise you might jeopardize the alignment of your pins. Using a firm grip or clamping pressure, slowly drill into your first mark and through to the bottom of the stacked scales. It's important to clean off the drill bit occasionally, as some materials will gunk it up.

50 With your tang still in place, take your marker and mark the first hole through the hole of the tang onto the handle material.

51 The best tool for drilling handle material is by far the drill press. A hand drill can also work, but it won't provide the accuracy that a drill press does. When selecting a drill bit, verify that it matches the size of the pins and the holes you've drilled into your blade's tang. Make sure that you use the correct type of drill bit for the type of material you're planning to drill. Brad-point drill bits are often my first choice when drilling most wood or synthetic materials. When using a powered drill, it's also important to maintain a proper drill speed for the given handle material.

52 After the first hole has been drilled, place one of the pins into the hole from the top and press it down into the bottom scale. Use some soft hammer taps or light pressure to get the pin in place if you have a tight fit. If that's still not working, don't force the pin, because this can lead to damaged handle material. Lightly hand-sand the pins to fit the hole.

53 Place the tang of the knife overtop the handle material again, sliding it over the pin and into alignment with the traced outline. Again, with a firm grip or clamping pressure on the handle material, slowly drill into the second hole using the tang itself as a template. Drill through the hole in the tang and through the stacked scales. At this stage, it's wise to tape off or wrap the edge of the blade; if your grip were to slip, you may end up with a high-speed knife carousel. Let me tell you, this is not a fun experience. Maintain proper security of the workpiece, don't forget to use protective equipment, and you should be just fine.

54 With the second hole drilled, pin it into place just like the first one. Repeat this process of drilling and pinning until you have a pin in place for each pinhole made in the tang. Once all the pins are in place, pat yourself on the back and move on to the rough-shaping of the handle. During this step, which is similar to the stock removal process (see page 76), you'll be cutting away the excess handle material outside of the guidelines that you created prior to drilling. Removing excess material can be done prior to or after the drilling process. I prefer to remove excess material after the pins are lined up; that way, if things end up becoming shifted, I still have some extra material as an insurance policy. However, I often remove a small amount of material prior to drilling if I'm feeling eager to see the handle take shape.

REMOVING WASTE MATERIAL

Again, the band saw is a fantastic tool for rough-cutting handle material, especially when cutting curves and contours. When using the band saw, excess material around a guideline can often be removed in a single pass. Handsaws will also work great when used properly.

Rough-shaping handle material will save you time later on when final shaping occurs after the handle material has been secured. I always recommend rough-shaping the handle material prior to glue-up because the handle can heat up quite a bit—especially when being shaped with a belt grinder or powered sander—and this could in turn ruin a bond that has been created with any epoxy.

55 A belt grinder can make fast work of shaving most materials when equipped with a sharp belt. Just be sure to wear your respirator to protect yourself from the dust.

FINISHING THE FRONT OF THE SCALES

Creating a guideline for the front of the handle.

After removing material up to the guideline, the front of the handle is looking nice and flush.

Once you have finished rough-shaping the handle, it's wise to apply final sanding to the front of the handle. A lot of full-tang knives feature a tapered finish at the front of the handle; now is a great time to go ahead and achieve that. This taper offers a smooth transition into the center of the handle, which is often wider, to create a palm swell that helps with **indexing** (gripping a knife).

The reasoning behind doing the final sanding and tapering on the front of the handle prior to glue-up is simple: It's difficult to reach these areas once the handle has been attached to the knife. Attempting to sand the front of the handle after it's been attached often results in marring up the surface of the steel, because the material you're sanding is sitting flush against it.

Final sanding generally means high-grit sanding. The process varies based on the handle material you're using and the type of finish you're hoping to achieve. The rule of thumb when finishing most materials is to start with a lower grit sandpaper and carefully work your way up in grits. When I'm working with wood I often start with about a 60 or 80 grit paper and work my way up through 100, 150, 220, and 320. I often finish the front of the handle with at least 400 grit paper prior to glue-up, but it's ideal to take it up to the highest grit that you plan to finish the rest of the handle with. With flashier knives, I'll sometimes sand up to around 800 or 1000 grit. When I'm working with synthetic materials such as Micarta, G10, or carbon fiber, I take a pretty similar sanding process, sometimes stopping shy of the very high grits.

At this point, the handle material has been drilled for holes, rough-shaped, and finished at the very front. Prior to permanently attaching all of the components, pull apart the stacked scales and pins because you'll be roughing up the insides of the scales. Roughing up the scales provides a better gripping surface for the epoxy (think ripping a Band-Aid off a hairy leg vs. ripping one off your forehead). You can rough up handle scales in the same fashion that you used to flatten them, but this time with a lower grit abrasive such as 80 grit. To go the extra mile, you can also create dimpling, which is done by drilling a bunch of small shallow holes inside the tanged portion of the scales. Just make sure to keep these holes inside the outline of the tang, otherwise they'll be noticeable when the handle is put back together.

Throughout the handle preparation process, you may end up taking the pins in and out. If the pins are tricky to get out, the use of a punch and hammer can be quite handy. Putting everything together to make sure it lines up well is what we knifemakers refer to as a **dry fit**. You don't want to realize that things are off after the handle's been covered in epoxy, because it makes a mess and you'll just have to clean it all up.

DRY FITTING THE COMPONENTS TOGETHER

If your handle construction isn't lining up, the reason why could be:

- an offset drilling surface,

- uneven scale thicknesses,

- debris that had been lodged between the scales prior to drilling,

- or maybe your scales are backwards and you just need to flip them over.

Sometimes it may seem like you've done everything right, but your pins just won't match up with the holes drilled into the tang. If they're only off by a small amount, you can sometimes open up the tang holes using a round needle file, but because your steel has been hardened it won't be fast work to take a file to it. Take your time during the handle preparation process because this is oftentimes the step that leads to the most mistakes for beginning knifemakers.

After a successful dry fit, the materials should be pulled apart and prepped for glue-up. I like to use masking tape to tape off the entirety of the blade; this keeps it clear of the epoxy. Epoxy won't ruin the blade, but it can be a hassle to clean off; I use acetone to remove unwanted epoxy. I also use masking tape to protect the finished front of the scales, because it can be tricky to get epoxy cleaned out of the corners where the handle meets the blade.

Epoxy

Epoxy is an adhesive that is used to hold handle material onto knife tangs. It's generally a two-part product—a resin and a hardener. When the resin and hardener are mixed, they react chemically and harden into a plastic-like material. All epoxies are designed to be mixed at a specified ratio, generally—but not always—one to one.

> **If the epoxy fails, then the knife fails.**

Consumer epoxies are usually described as either a quick-curing 5-minute epoxy or a slow-curing 60-minute epoxy. On average, quick-curing epoxy uses a hardener known as mercaptan, and the slow-curing epoxy often uses a hardener known as polyamide. A slower curing epoxy often makes for a stronger overall bond. Epoxy is temperature sensitive, and the rule of thumb is that the colder it is, the longer it will take for the epoxy to cure.

Regardless of the type of epoxy you use, surface preparation is the key to success. Make sure that the surfaces of the workpieces are completely oil and grease free. You also want to have as much **tooth** as possible, meaning you want a rough surface, because a very smooth surface will not grip the epoxy as well. You can roughen up both the knife tang and the handle material with a lower-grit sandpaper.

It's crucial to use good stuff because if the epoxy fails, then the knife fails. Depending on the style of knifemaking you are approaching, epoxy might not be completely necessary. This may be the case with ancient methods such as Japanese sword making. But most modern knifemaking techniques benefit from the use of epoxy.

When applying clamps to joints filled with epoxy, it's important to manage your pressure correctly. You should get some **squeeze out**, or epoxy leaving the joints when pressure is added, but too much pressure may result in too much epoxy loss. Cranking down too hard on the clamps can cause your joint to ultimately end up weaker due to the loss of epoxy, so keep that in mind when gluing up components.

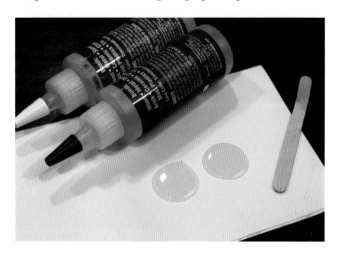

Making a Hidden-Tang Knife Handle

Creating a handle for a hidden-tang knife is quite a different process from your standard full-tang handle. There are many ways to go about making a hidden-tang handle, many of which incorporate multiple pieces and require much more attention to detail in order to achieve a successful fit up. In its simplest form, a hidden-tang handle can be made from a simple block of material and some careful fitting to insert the tang.

In order to mechanically secure the handle to the tang, a pin can be added, much like in a full-tang knife handle. Another layer of security is to extend the tang through the back of the handle material and use a ball-peen hammer to mushroom or spread the tip of the tang over top of the handle material. Peening the tang works best if the steel is soft. Using a handheld torch, you can heat up the tip of the tang. Be cautious of accidentally reheating the edged portion of the knife: this may result in a ruined heat treat. To really get a grasp on things, you'll need to understand the different styles of hidden tang handle constructions.

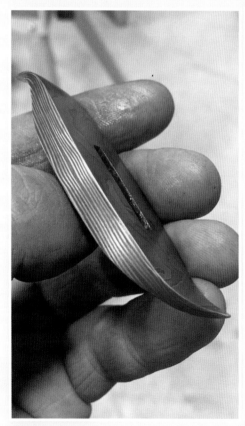

A guard all polished and ready for assembly.

Handle components being dry-fitted prior to glue-up.

This guard has been successfully fitted to the shoulders of the blade.

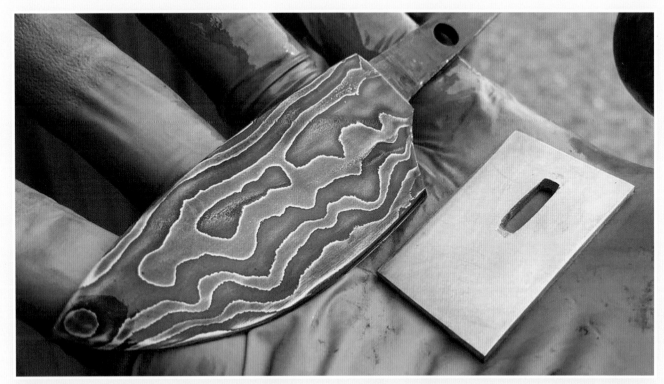

Bolsters are most commonly used on hidden-tang handles. They slide onto the tang and rest on the shoulders of the blade. The rest of the handle is then slid into place and rests against the bolster.

BOLSTERS & GUARDS

Oftentimes, hidden-tang knives will incorporate a bolster. A **bolster** is a strong piece of material, usually metal, that is used at the front of the handle for added strength. The bolster is a sort of collar that is used to protect the end grain of a wooden or delicate piece of handle material.

A bolster can also be made from two pieces similar to knife scales that are attached to a full-tang handle. Bolsters can even be integral with the rest of the knife, but this is a more advanced forging technique that I won't recommend to beginner knifemakers. A bolster that protects the user's hand from slipping forward and onto the blade is called a **guard**, which is created by extending the bolster in height and/or width to stand farther out from the tang than the rest of the handle.

A large hidden-tang bowie knife featuring a Damascus guard, rosewood handle, partially serrated edge, and a leather sheath.

In order for a guard or bolster to seat properly on the tang, the tang needs to be tapered in both width and thickness. The tang's thickest and widest spots should be at the shoulder where the tang meets the rest of the blade. The thinnest and most narrow spots should be at the very back of the tang. The bolster or guard needs to fit the tang very accurately; otherwise, when slid into place against the shoulders, you will have visible gaps. Fitting a bolster or guard is a meticulous process that requires patience. There are numerous ways to go about the task, but drilling and filing are by far the most common techniques.

A The height and width of the tang where it meets the shoulders need to be measured and transferred onto the face of the bolster or guard.

B Select a drill bit that is smaller than the thickness of the tang, and then drill a series of holes in a straight line that fit within the measurement on the workpiece. To accurately drill the holes, make sure to begin with a straight line. I recommend using a marking knife rather than a pencil for a more precise line. Use a punch to mark each hole; this will help keep you on track. It is also wise to space out the holes by about 1/32 in. (0.8 mm) because this will help prevent the drill bit from slipping into the neighboring hole during drilling.

C Using either a small file or needle file, carefully open up the holes, joining them into one continuous slot. The width of the slot should be a few thousandths of an inch smaller than the shoulder of the blade; this way the taper on the tang to the shoulder will hide the slot when the bolster or guard is assembled. Filing a slotted fitting takes patience; expect a lot of back and forth filing and test fitting, until your guard or bolster starts to seat nicely near the shoulders.

If you make any small mistakes, just remember that there will only be one visible face on the bolster or guard. The backside will be hidden against the rest of the handle material. So if you do mess up, you can flip the bolster around to hide a small blemish or scratch.

D Once about 90 percent of the fitting work has been done, you can achieve an extra tight fit by press-fitting the guard or bolster. To press-fit the guard or bolster, place the blade into a vise, with the shoulders exposed and the tang pointed up. To protect your blade, make sure to wrap it with tape or a soft material of sorts. Slide the guard or bolster into place, then slip a piece of pipe over the tang so that it rests on the fitting and extends past the back of the tang. Lightly tap the pipe with a hammer. This will press the fitting nicely up onto the shoulders.

> *In order to create a strong hidden-tang handle, the tang of the knife should extend at least more than halfway into the block.*

SLOTTING THE BLOCK

It's important to square up your **block** (see page 128 for definition) before moving forward with this step—easily done with a belt grinder, band saw, or rasps. Then, just like slotting a guard or bolster, the block needs to be slotted to fit the tang. Slotting the block is a much different process than slotting a guard or bolster.

In order to create a strong hidden-tang handle, the tang of the knife should extend at least more than halfway into the block. Just like with slotting a guard or bolster, you'll want to take your time and keep accuracy in mind when slotting the block. However, you don't need to be as critical with your slotting, because there will not be any visible gaps—the guard or bolster will be capping them off.

A drill press is a great tool to get started slotting a block. While a hand drill can be used as well, it requires more focus to achieve accuracy.

A Start off as if you were slotting a guard or bolster—by measuring the width and thickness of the tang where it meets the shoulder, then transferring that measurement to the block. Then measure the depth of the tang to the height of the drill bit, as you won't want to drill any deeper than needed.

B Drilling a series of three holes in a straight line, with the center hole being the deepest, is common practice. You can make the holes slightly larger than the thickness of the tang. After drilling the initial holes at the drill press, the block can be secured into a vice and a hand drill can be used to wiggle around and enlarge the inside of the hole until it has reach the proper size to accept the tang.

C Using a **broach**, which is a small cutting tool with a series of teeth, enlarge the slot within the block. Another method of enlarging a slot in a block is to burn it to size by heating and inserting the tang so it will burn the slot to a perfect fit. When heating a tang, be wary of the heat-treated edge of the blade—too much heat may damage the temper.

Securing a Pin

A common method of securing the tang to the handle is to add a pin, just like in a full-tang handle construction. This requires a few precise measurements in order to get a proper alignment.

A With the tang inserted into the handle block, mark exactly where the top and bottom of the tang rest. If you're using a guard or bolster, first mark the tang so that you only insert the tang up to the point at which it meets the guard or bolster. With the top and bottom marks in place, transfer them onto the face of the block using a square.

B Remove the tang from the handle block and place it on the face of the block so that it rests between the marks that have been made. At this point the tang should be resting on the face of the block, aligned with the slot inside. If you are using a guard or bolster, it should be placed onto the tang at this time.

C1 Transfer a mark through the hole of the tang and onto the face of the block. Using a drill press is the most accurate way to drill the pinhole. Make sure you have a flat surface and be sure that your block is secure, and then drill the pinhole at the mark that you made. It's important to use a drill bit that matches the size of the pin you'll be using as well at the size of the pinhole drilled into the tang. Chamfer your pin for ease of entrance into the pinhole.

C2 To get an extra tight fit, you can shift your mark and drill your pinhole a few thousandths of an inch toward the back of the block. This will result in a very slight offset between the hole in the tang and the hole in the handle block. A well-chamfered pin will find its way into the tang hole and, with some pressure, actually pull the components together. If you were to move your hole slightly forward onto the handle block, however, this would result in pulling the components apart.

D If your holes aren't in alignment to seat together properly, you may consider using a **needle file** to elongate the hole in the tang until it lines up with the hole in the handle block. If the hole in the tang is farther forward than the hole in the block, another fix would be to very carefully remove some material from the front of the block until the holes match up. Removing material from the front of the block can be tricky and I avoid it whenever I can.

Spacers

The use of spacers is quite common in hidden-tang assembly. Spacers often sit between the bolster or guard and the rest of the handle material. They are made in the same fashion as a bolster or a guard, though they don't require the same precision when it comes to slotting because they won't show any visible gaps.

The purpose of spacers is often aesthetic but can help to shift handle material if pinholes are out of alignment. Spacers made from a compressible material such as leather, cork, or birch allow some compression to help correct the misalignment of the pinholes. Compressible material is also nice when working with a pommel, because when the pommel is attached you will be able to observe the material compress, proving you have a tight fit up.

POMMELS

Hidden-tang knife handles often have pommels. The back of the handle is frequently referred to as the butt, while a pommel is a separate piece placed at the butt of the knife to reinforce it. Pommels are most commonly made from metal and often pair with a matching guard or bolster. A pommel is secured to the handle in one of two ways. The first and most traditional method of securing a pommel is to drill through it, as if slotting the handle block for the tang.

A Rather than drilling multiple holes, drill just one hole, using a drill bit that matches the thickness of the back end of the tang. In order for this method to work, the tang must extend past the handle rather than stopping short, as it would in the previous technique.

B The back of the tang is then ground or filed until it closely matches the round profile of the hole in the pommel. A belt grinder is a great tool to help round the back of the tang; I recommend using a mid to higher grit belt to prevent removing more material than needed. Single-cut files are a great option for material reduction as well. This process is similar to fitting a guard or bolster, in the sense that there is a lot of back-and-forth filing and checking.

C After you have achieved a good fit between the tang and the pommel, you'll want to finish up preparing your components for glue-up prior to attaching the pommel, because once it's attached it won't be easily removed.

D When the time comes and you're ready to attach the pommel, place your blade into a vise, tang aiming up, and slide the pommel over the tang. The pommel should seat against the rest of the handle material. If you're planning to use epoxy, be sure to apply it prior to attaching the pommel (more instruction on epoxy to come, see page 154). The tang should be cut so that all there is protruding from the back of the pommel is a tang length equivalent to the thickness of the tang.

E1 Using a ball-peen hammer, proceed to hammer over the tang as you would a rivet. This will cause the tang to mushroom and spread over the top of the pommel, making it impossible to remove. You'll be left with a small steel nub similar to a rivet.

E2 To avoid the look of a nub, there's another way to go about this that will result in a cleaner finish. You'll need to chamfer the hole at the back of the pommel. This way, when the tang is hammered, it will fill the chamfer rather than spread across the outer surface of the pommel. Excess material can be ground off and flushed up with the back of the pommel.

Alternative: Threaded Pommel

Another common way to secure a pommel takes some of the same steps as the above technique. The difference is that after the hole has been drilled and the tang has been rounded to match, the tang and the pommel hole can both be threaded to match. This will cause them to work as a nut and bolt. When you have moved onto the glue-up and final fitting stage, the threaded assembly will allow the pommel to work as a clamp securing the rest of the material tightly to the shoulders of the tang. With this method, the hole in the pommel can also be stopped short of going through, resulting in an invisible joint.

Applying Epoxy to a Full-Tang Handle

When working with epoxy, I'm always sure to have some disposable rubber gloves because this stuff can be hard to clean off, and it just doesn't feel great to have it all over your hands. I also prefer to work over some wax paper—this keeps my components from sticking to my work surface, and it also gives me a place to mix epoxy on.

The type of epoxy you use is completely up to you. As I say on page 147, slower curing epoxies are generally stronger than the faster curing five-minute epoxies. Each epoxy will have its own instructions and they should be followed accurately. Most epoxies are a two-step product that includes a resin and a hardener, and more often that not, they will be mixed at a ratio of one-to-one.

If your blade isn't taped up already, now would be the time because it'll save you from cleaning off excess epoxy if it gets on the blade.

Materials you will need for glue-up, clockwise from left: clamps, popsicle stick, two-part epoxy, latex or rubber gloves, wax paper to cover your work surface.

56 When everything is in line, dry-fit your handle components to make sure you have a successful fit-up. Once you're happy with the way things look, disassemble your components because it's time for glue-up.

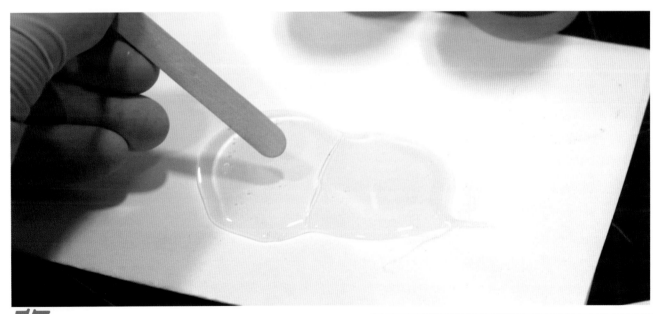

57 Make sure to mix your epoxy on a clean and, better yet, non-stick surface, such as plastic or wax paper (I prefer wax paper). If the surface you mix on is dirty, you may pick up some unwanted particles that make their way into the handle. Mixing is easily done with a popsicle stick; it can be found at about any craft store and is often pretty cheap. When mixing your epoxy, it's important to make sure the resin and hardener are fully mixed prior to applying to the handle components.

Applying Epoxy to a Full-Tang Handle

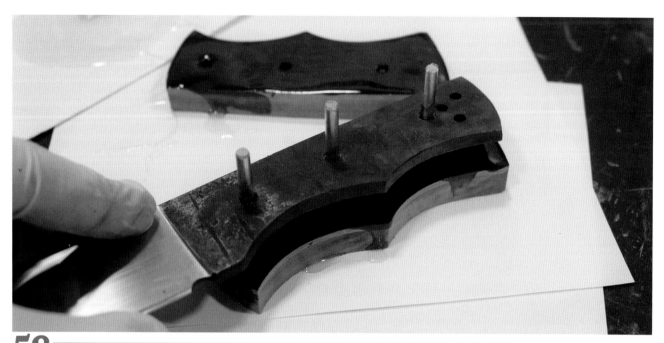

58 When applying epoxy to a full-tang knife, start by spreading it across the inside faces of both scales. Lightly apply it to each pin, and follow up by inserting the pins into one of the scales. Once the pins have been inserted into the first scale, the knife tang can be slid over the top of the pins until it rests into the epoxy on the scale.

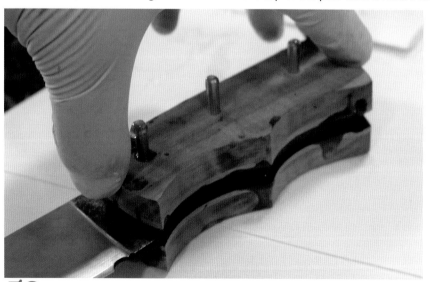

59 Slide the second scale down over the pins until it rests on the other components. If you find it difficult to pull all the components together, use a small clamp over the scales to help force things into alignment; just be careful and take your time so you don't damage or break anything. Verify that all the pins are pushed far enough through on either side of the handle. If you have to, tap them until they are sitting evenly.

Keeping a small hammer nearby to help lightly tap pins into place can be very handy. I've also found that utilizing a small **arbor press** can very efficiently press pins into place, and it's less violent than hammering the pins. The arbor press I own was sourced at a flea market years ago for a great price, and I still use it all the time.

60 Once the components are all fastened, use clamps to hold the material tightly together until the epoxy dries. When applying clamps to the material, you don't want to crank them on too tight because you may squeeze too much glue out of the joints, resulting in a weaker assembly. Also keep in mind that epoxy is a heat-sensitive material; it won't set up properly if left in a very cold environment.

61 Using acetone is a great way to remove "squeeze out," or excess epoxy, before it has fully cured onto the blade. Cleaning up the junction between the blade and the handle is best done earlier than later, as removing hardened epoxy can be quite difficult.

Applying Epoxy to a Hidden-Tang Handle

Applying epoxy to a hidden-tang knife isn't much different. You'll want to fill the entire slot of the handle block with epoxy and spread epoxy well between all the other components. Filling the slot with epoxy can be a bit messy, but it's best to use too much rather than too little. If the epoxy oozes out of any pinholes, it's a good sign that you've used enough.

Assemble the pieces and, if needed, use light hammer taps or careful pressure to get any pins into place. Make sure any pins are far enough through the handle material on either side.

If you're attaching a pommel (see page 153), now is the time to do so. If you've achieved a tight fit, you will not need any clamping pressure. Make sure to let the epoxy fully cure in a warm environment.

CHAPTER 9: SHAPING THE HANDLE

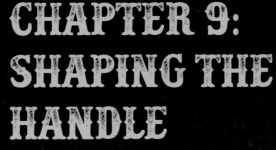

Shaping the handle has to be my favorite step in the knifemaking process. It's here that you get to actually feel the knife in your hand and visualize all the hard work that you put in to get the knife to this point in the process. A handle needs to fit your hand well, just like a shoe to your foot.

If the handle is not profiled well, you'll end up with **hot spots**, or areas that cause discomfort when you use the knife. The way you shape your handle depends on the size of your hands and the tasks that you will perform with the knife. And the tools you use sometimes depend on the type of handle material you'll be shaping.

A couple of the steps below are more directed toward shaping a full-tang knife handle because it features an exposed spine. Other than that, everything covered in this chapter is usable information whether you're shaping a hidden- or full-tang handle.

Shaping Prior to Glue-Up

A hidden-tang handle can be shaped, or at least rough-shaped, prior to glue-up. You might also consider pinning two scales of a full-tang knife handle together to shape them prior to glue-up as well, but keep in mind that the pins will be an obstacle during shaping. Rounding the edges over on a handle will also make things difficult for a clamp to get a proper grip, which isn't much of an issue for hidden-tang handles because they don't necessarily require any clamping.

Squaring Up the Handle

Before you begin rounding over any edges or creating curves and contours, focus on squaring up the handle. If you can first develop an evenly squared handle, it will help you to stay consistent during the shaping process.

Create a squared handle by flattening the sides and edges of the hand material. Flat sides will allow the handle to sit in a level position against the belt grinder, which will help in consistency when flipping the workpiece from one side to the other.

62 If you have attached your handle to your tang with pins, the first thing I recommend doing is removing any excess pin material that protrudes from the handle. Pin material can easily be removed with the use of a hacksaw or an angle grinder with a cutoff wheel. A band saw is also capable of this task. My personal preference is to secure my blade into a vise and use either a hacksaw or an angle grinder to cut off those proud-standing pins. I remove the pins so that I'm left with about ⅛ in. (3 mm) of pin material sticking out, and then I finish things off by flushing up the pins against the flat platen of a belt grinder. This last step can also be accomplished with a file.

Go Easy on the Belt Grinder

If you have a lot of excess pin material to remove, for example, more than ¼ in. (6 mm), I would avoid grinding it all away using a belt grinder. The friction that a belt grinder generates transfers a lot of heat into the pin material, and that heat can actually destroy the bond that the epoxy has created to hold the pin in place. Remember when we discussed ruining a steel's heat treat by overheating it (see page 116)? Well, we also need to be careful about overheating and ruining an epoxy's bond.

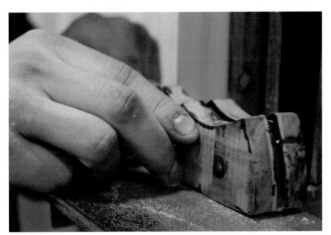

63 After excess pin material has been removed and flushed up with the surface of the handle material, it's crucial to flatten both sides of the handle material. You'll want the sides flat and level, because after this step you will be flushing up the edges of the material until the spine is exposed around the entire perimeter. To flatten the sides it can help to first make a few measurements from the spine to use as a reference point. The best tools to use are belt grinders or disc grinders that can fit the entire handle against a platen at once. This will offer very exact results and will quickly remove any unevenness in the handle. My personal method of flushing up and flattening the sides of my handle material is to press the material vertically against the platen of my 2 in. (51 mm) wide belt grinder. This way the entire side of the handle is sanded at once.

Hand Tool Alternative

This step can also be done with files, rasps, or a low grit piece of sandpaper, but without the use of power tools will require more patience. I recommend buying large, low grit sanding discs. They have an adhesive backing and can be easily attached to any flat, sturdy surface. Using a sanding disc or a piece of sandpaper on top of a flat surface such as a piece of glass is a popular choice among knifemakers. The handle can then be pressed down flat and continuously pulled over the top of the disc to create a flat surface. (This trick can also be used to flatten up handle scales prior to attaching them to the tang.)

64 To verify that the handle material is flat and level, use a caliper or measuring device to check the dimensions from scale to scale at multiple points around the handle. If you have high spots, mark them with a pencil and continue flattening using more pressure over those areas. You don't need to be deadly accurate since this is a handmade knife. But the more accurate you are, the better it will look and feel in the end.

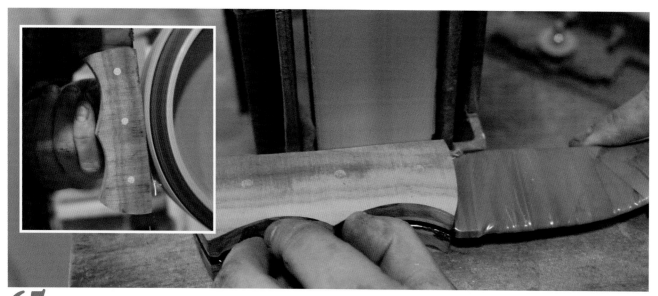

65 When you are shaping a full-tang knife handle, you have to flush up the edges where the handle material is attached to the tang. Because the sides have now been flattened and leveled, you can place them on top of a tool rest against a belt grinder or disc grinder. If the sides of the handle are square, and the tool rest you're using it on is square, you will be able to produce square edges as well.

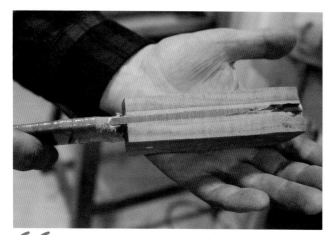

66 At this point you want to remove material around the edges until you begin exposing the steel tang sandwiched between the scales. You only need to remove just enough handle material to be able to flush it up with the tang. If you're using a powered grinder, just remember not to overheat the steel tang.

Hand Tool Alternative

Having a belt grinder or a disc sander with a solid tool rest makes this process a piece of cake, but you can get by just fine with a **rasp** or a **file**. If you're using a rasp or a file to shape your handle material, keep in mind that most of these tools only cut on the push and not on the pull. Don't go crazy with your pressure because too much may lead to cracking or chip outs in your handle material.

I strongly recommend a high quality **cabinet rasp**, specifically a **half-round cabinet rasp**. A cabinet rasp is essentially a good quality medium-grit rasp. These can be a bit pricey, and, as a beginner, it's fine to use cheap stuff. Just know that cheaper tools won't work as well or last as long as a quality tool. Flea markets are a great place to find rasps and files.

Making the Handle Comfortable

This Damascus knife features a hand-filed spine, and a handle made from ironwood, African blackwood, and turquoise.

Now that you have squared things up and exposed the tang (assuming you're shaping a full-tang handle), it's time to get creative and turn this block of a handle into something ergonomic and comfortable in the hand. Start by planning out the flow of how you'd like your handle to be profiled. Do want a wider handle, or would you prefer something thinner? How about adding a taper, or some grooving for your fingers? You can figure this out beforehand, or you can just get started and see how things go. A lot of times I'll just jump in and feel the progress as I move along, making decisions along the way as I see fit. But starting off with a simple plan can be wise, because as soon as you remove too much material from the handle, you either have to live with it or start over.

Shaping a handle is one of those things that can go extremely well or extremely wrong in a matter of seconds. So throughout this process, just make sure to take your time and accept the fact that mistakes happen. If it makes you feel better, I've already lost count of the number of handles that I've completely butchered.

It's important to be able to **index** a handle. What this means is that, without looking, you need to be able to know where the blade is just by how your hand fits in the handle. There are many ways to achieve a nice index, but most commonly it requires the use of tapers and swells.

Tapering a handle from the butt to the front, the butt being the thickest point, is a very simple and effective way to improve the indexing of a handle. A **swell** is essentially a smooth hump of handle material that's created by making a low spot on either side and then ramping those low spots until they meet in the middle of the high spot between them. Swells are a way to improve the ergonomics of a handle as well as prevent hot spots when in use. An example of a swell would be the way that the butt end of an axe handle widens to improve comfort and prevent slipping. Oftentimes knife handles incorporate a swell designed to fill the center of the palm. Some handles also feature a swell at the butt end to keep the hand positioned at the center of the handle. Tapers and swells make up the overall contours of a handle.

I personally enjoy incorporating swells into my knife handle designs. They provide great grip and they make a handle very easy to index. Half-round rasps are excellent tools to use when sculpting swells on your handles. The use of a contact wheel on a belt grinder is another fantastic choice due to its curvature. Creating swells with flat cutting tools will prove to be quite difficult, however.

67 The classic "coke bottle" shape is a very popular design that is based off the shape of a bottle.

68 You can shape your handle from a squared-up block down to a finished profile using only a file or a belt grinder. You can also save yourself some time by first sketching the profile onto the edges of the handle, and then use a band saw to remove the unwanted material outside of your sketch lines. I personally enjoy using only rasps and contact wheels to rough-shape my knife handles. As you start to get in some practice, you'll begin to develop your own personal preferences.

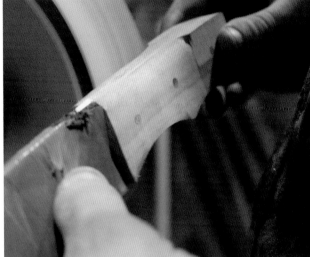

69 When you begin to sculpt a handle, you first need to figure out where you'd like to place any swells. Design and contours are completely up to you as the maker. Create a swell by first shaping away a low spot and then gradually connecting it back to a high spot. A half-round rasp is an excellent choice, along with a contact wheel on a belt grinder. Smooth transitions are key in avoiding hot spots while the knife is in use.

70 Round over the edges of the handle by blending the face into the material alongside the tang. A rasp or the slack portion of a belt grinder are both ideal tools for this job. Another trick is to secure your blade into a vise (provide some padding to avoid blade damage), turn a sanding belt inside out, and, holding either side of the belt, begin to pull the belt back and forth over the top of the handle. This is an easy way to achieve a pretty even and accurate profile.

Making the Handle Comfortable   **165**

Finishing the Knife

If you've made it this far, congratulations, because from here on out you're sailing much calmer waters. Once you have achieved the shape that you want, you need to take your handle up the scale of sandpaper grits to achieve a smooth and polished finish.

FINISH SANDING

Certain synthetic handle materials may not require the same amount of high grit sanding as many natural materials do, but it doesn't hurt to bring them up a little higher than needed. When you stop noticing any improvements in the handle material's finish, it's a good sign that the sanding and polishing is close to finished.

The sandpaper grit that you start with should be just lower than or equal to the grit you used to hand-sand the handle in the rough-shaping process—about 220 grit in my case, usually. I often begin finish sanding at a grit of 150–220. The reason for stepping back in grit is just to guarantee that I have an equal removal of scratches at the lower grit prior to stepping back up. If I do my rough-shaping with a rasp and a file, which is much courser than a 220 grit belt, I'll start hand-sanding with a lower grit paper, such as 80 grit.

When sanding, focus on blending sharp corners or junctions around swells and tapers. If you have any metal handle pins, make sure to take your time sanding them very well, because leftover scratches or rough spots are very obvious in a polished metal pin. The goal when sanding is to remove all scratches left behind by the previous grit. This is essentially the same approach that you'd take as if you were hand-sanding a blade to achieve a satin finish.

You can achieve a nice polish on an exposed full tang and spine by sanding with the direction of the tang. When sanding down the tang in a full-tang

71 Once the material has been rounded, begin sanding to guarantee that all sharp corners or edges are smooth and blended. This is the final step in the rough-shaping process, and I prefer to use a slacked portion of the belt grinder. Pushing the handle material into a slacked belt allows the belt to form around the material and provide a better blend than it would if you used a flat platter or contact wheel. Avoid using a rasp at this point, but flat and half-round files will do great. The primary goal here is to begin to smooth things out and prepare for finish sanding and polishing in the next step.

handle, blend the polish into the spine by occasionally sanding it all together. This will give the steel tang and spine a nice shine.

My hand-sanding grit progression after rough-shaping is generally 220, 320, 400, and then 600.

You can bring your handle to a higher grit, such as 800, 1000, or even up to 2000, but I find 600 to be a great stopping point. From my experience 600 grit is a sweet spot between a nice polish and a handle that is too smooth to grip in wet conditions. I've noticed that handles with close to a mirror polish will not offer much friction and are more slippery.

Oiling

Once I reach about 400 grit in my hand-sanding process, I oil the handle. This is only really necessary for wooden handles and some other natural handle materials.

Continue to oil the handle until it no longer absorbs the oil. If your handle material is well stabilized, it won't soak up much oil. If you're working with an unstabilized piece of wood, you can leave your handle to soak in a cup of oil overnight. This isn't a crucial step to take, but it's a great way to let the oil completely penetrate the wood. Plus, it makes for a much longer-lasting handle that won't dry out or require re-oiling anytime soon.

72 Start sanding handle material back and forth, changing direction frequently to avoid creating deep channels with the lower grit paper. Once I've moved up to a higher grit, such as 320, I'll begin to keep a consistent sanding direction down the length of the handle.

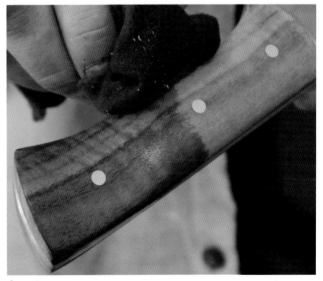

73 After reaching 400 grit, heavily coat wooden handles with a boiled linseed oil. Many knifemakers will use other oils such as tung oil or mineral oil, and these may work great, but I always swear by boiled linseed oil.

Wet-Sand up to 600 Grit

After oiling the handle, step back and start to hand-sand at the grit that you left off at. If you're going along with my technique, you'll start sanding at 400 grit again. You don't need to let the oil dry prior to handling; in fact, sanding with oil or **wet-sanding** is a great way to create an even smoother finish. The dust removed from the handle material will mix with the oil, creating a sort of muddy mixture that will aid in filling any pores in the handle material.

Get the surface of the handle material sitting flush and uniform at 400 grit, and then step up to 600 grit. Sanding with lower grits should ultimately take longer than sanding with higher grits. As you move up in grits, the material will get smoother and the scratches or sanding marks will get smaller and become easier to remove.

Clean the Knife and Oil the Blade

Once all of the hand-sanding has been finished, give your knife a good cleaning using some warm water and a little bit of dish soap. I've found that using a **toothbrush** is a great way to clean a knife. After you have cleaned the blade, be sure to dry it completely and lightly oil the blade to prevent any rust from forming. I always prefer to use food-safe oil on my blades. That way, if I choose to process food or meat using the knife, I don't need to bother cleaning the oil off first. A couple of great oils to use are **olive oil** or **canola oil**, and you can also purchase specialty oils designed for use on knife blades and other carbon steel tools.

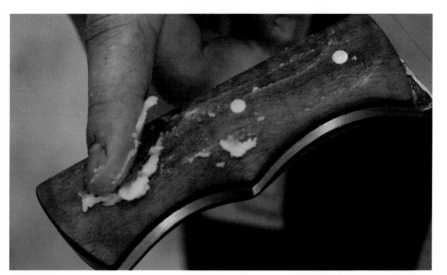

Wax the Handle

Once you've achieved a cleaned knife and oiled blade, you'll want to take one more step to finish the handle. I've tried many handle-finishing techniques, and my favorite by far is to apply wax, and buff it in by hand with a soft cloth.

A little bit of wax paste applied to a wooden handle will provide a lot of protection from the elements. I make my own basic yet extremely effective wax paste out of boiled linseed oil and beeswax.

74 Take a small finger and spread a thin coat over the entire handle. Use a clean, soft rag or towel to help spread the wax, and then buff the wax into the handle by quickly moving the rag over the handle as if you were shining a pair of boots. Wipe away any excess wax when you're finished buffing.

My Wax Paste Recipe

There are many waxes on the market designed to protect wood, but I've been making my own wax for quite some time. You can make a pretty basic yet extremely effective wax paste out of boiled linseed oil and beeswax.

1 To follow my recipe, start by melting down some beeswax. You can do this on a stove top but I've also found myself melting wax in my shop using a heat gun; just be sure to use a metal or heat-resistant container.

2 Once the wax has become liquid, pour in some boiled linseed oil. The more oil you add, the looser the mixture will be. I've found a good mixture to be about 1 part beeswax and 1½ parts boiled linseed oil. You can experiment with different ratios, waxes, or oils; just be sure to keep safety in mind when using a heat source and mixing chemicals.

3 Use a stirring stick to mix the oil with the wax for a couple minutes until they blend well. Pour the mixture into a container for later use. I recommend a container with a lid to prevent the wax from drying out. This mixture will also work great to protect leather products such as knife sheaths.

FINISHED!

At this point the handle is completely done, the blade is completely done, and you've got a knife that will last a lifetime and then some. It felt great when I finished my very first knife, but what's great is that I still get that feeling today every time I finish a knife. This is a very rewarding craft and like most things, you get out of it what you put into it. Making your own knife is awesome, but being able to use that knife to successfully complete tasks is very satisfying. There's a lot of pride in making and using your own tools, and any knifemaker discovers that pretty early on.

CHAPTER 10: PROPER KNIFE CARE & MAINTENANCE

A handmade knife can become an heirloom that is passed down for many years. If it's built well, it will outlast and outperform those cheap production knives that we all despise. But in order for any knife to live a long and fulfilling life, it needs to be taken care of properly. This means proper cleaning, proper sharpening, and, most importantly, proper use.

A well-made knife may be a showcase-quality piece of art, but it will also be tough and resilient to the uses it was designed to encounter. What I mean is that a skinning knife is not often designed to also chop down a tree, nor is a large machete designed to be thrown for target practice. More often than not, if a quality knife breaks, it is because it was asked to do something it was not designed for. When using a knife, keep in mind that an axe, saw, pry bar, and hammer are completely different tools.

Cleaning & Oiling

With a carbon steel knife, you'll have to be wary of rust. The best way to avoid rust is to keep the blade well cleaned and oiled. After every use, I recommend cleaning the entire blade and handle using **dish detergent** and **warm water**. You can also use a **sponge** or a **toothbrush** to help scrub any dirt and get a deeper clean. Afterwards, immediately dry off the knife—if you allow the water to settle on the steel, it will cause it to rust.

OILING THE STEEL

Once the knife has been cleaned, all of the steel components (blade, handle pins, and visible tang) should be lightly oiled. My advice is to use a food-grade oil such as canola, olive, or sunflower oil. This way, if your knife encounters food at all on the trail, you don't have to be concerned about tainting the food with harmful oils.

Oil designed specifically for knives or guns is a great choice if you plan to be storing the knife for a period of time. Oil should be used sparingly because a thick oil coat can attract a layer of dust. Also keep in mind that some oils may cause the blade to stain or force a patina. This isn't necessarily harmful to the blade, but it may change the look of the steel.

REMOVING SURFACE RUST

If you notice that your blade has picked up a little bit of rust, it's best to deal with it right away. A little bit of surface rust can easily turn into deep pitting in the steel and can over time ruin the functionality of a knife.

An example of pitting probably caused by rust on the face of an old axe head.

Removing surface rust is a pretty simple process, especially for a knifemaker. There are a few ways to go about this, but I avoid power tools. If you have very light rusting, it can sometimes be removed using a **toothbrush** and **toothpaste**. The toothpaste has some grit to it that allows it to break down the rust when it's scrubbed in. You may also try scrubbing the blade with some high grit **steel wool** along with **soapy water**.

DEEPER RUST

For rust that is a bit deeper, take a step back to when you finished the bevels. For example, if you hand-sanded your bevels, move back to that 400 or 600 grit paper and lightly go over the bevel again. If you used a buffing wheel, try a couple passes with a higher grit to remove the rust. Just keep in mind that, when using power tools, you need to be cautious and avoid ruining your heat treat. This means keep cooling the blade in water as you move along.

Honing & Sharpening

Sharpening a blade involves removing tiny pieces of steel from either side until the sides meet to create a very fine edge. If you sharpen your blade after every use, you'll eventually notice the effects of over-sharpening: your blade will become thinner and thinner over time. If you notice the edge starting to dull after heavy use, just hone the edge with a ceramic rod or a leather strop (see page 123). Proper and continuous honing will keep your edge keen and functioning properly. A knife that is well honed will not need constant heavy sharpening. In fact, I only truly sharpen my personal knives a few times each year.

If your knife encounters some seriously heavy use and dulls out quite a bit, you may be required to re-sharpen the edge. I recommend taking out the old whetstone and start off on the higher grit side. As covered in pages 122–125, do about ten to twenty passes on either side of the edge and finish things off by honing with a ceramic rod or a leather strop.

Over the course of a knife's life, it's possible that it will develop a **chip**. This can be the result of several variables, including dropping the knife, a faulty heat treat, or general misuse. If the chip is small, you may be able to work it out by re-sharpening the blade, starting with a lower grit and moving your way up through the honing process. If this doesn't do the trick, you may need to step back to the grinder or file that you used to initially form the micro bevel and re-grind it with a slightly wider angle. Taking out a

chip is sometimes a troubleshooting process, but it's something that every seasoned knifemaker has dealt with at least a few times.

The better you become at knifemaking, the less you'll have to deal with things like chips. Just remember that if the edge easily dents or rolls over, the steel is too soft. A chip, on the other hand, might be an indication that the blade is too hard. Continue to perfect your heat treat and you'll be in good shape.

Knife Safety

A sharp knife is a safe knife. This is a tip that I picked up a long time ago and I've continued to follow. A dull knife requires a lot of force to complete a task when, really, the tool should be doing the work for you. Imagine sitting down and carving with a dull knife, trying to force the blade through a piece of walnut. It takes all of your effort to cut through and you eventually skip off the wood and the blade stabs into your thigh. A dull knife may be dull, but a dull knife is still pointy. Let's say you hit your femoral artery; now you're in big trouble unless you can fashion a tourniquet and get help quickly. This is a worst-case scenario, but it happens more than it should.

Speaking from Personal Experience

I was wilderness camping in Michigan's Upper Peninsula with my brother and our friend in the winter. Long story short, I was chopping wood, and the axe hopped off a log and chopped through my boot, into my anklebone. We ended up packing out. I was able to get my wound stitched up about four hours later. My advice to anyone using a knife, or any tool for that matter, is to take your time and give your full attention to every task you perform. Multitasking may seem like a way to save time, but an injury will set you back further than you'd expect.

Handle Maintenance

If your knife has a wooden handle, the handle will need some oil every so often. It may be a well-stabilized piece of wood, but over time the material can begin to dry out. The best way to avoid this is to take some oil—my personal favorite being linseed oil—and apply it heavily to the handle material. Continue to apply the oil until it no longer wants to soak into the wood.

If you're not sure if your handle needs to be oiled, sprinkle some water droplets onto the wood and check to see if the handle absorbs the water in or if the water sits on top. If it absorbs water, apply oil because that's exactly what you're preventing. If it has been a long time since you've oiled the handle, you may need to go back and sand off any raised grain using a high grit sandpaper.

If the handle ever needs more attention than a little bit of oil, you can always refer to the previous steps you've taken to make and finish it. I find myself oiling, waxing, and buffing my knife handles a few times a year, and that's just about all the maintenance that it takes for a knife handle that's used fairly heavily.

Use cardboard and tape to make a slipcover for the blade.

Storing a Knife

An issue that I see quite a bit among knife owners is improper storage of a knife. This may not seem like much of an issue, but it actually is. When picturing a knife you probably think of its strength, durability, and performance, but a knife is also very vulnerable to a number of variables when it isn't taken care of or stored correctly. To make things simple, if you take care of your knife, it will take care of you.

Many knife owners consider a sheath to be the best place to store a knife, and this is true if you're out on the trail or actually using the knife. But if the hunting season is over and you are putting your knife away for a while, *Long storage in a sheath can actually damage a knife.* long storage in a sheath can actually damage a knife. This is because a sheath, whether it be leather or Kydex, will block moisture from escaping the knife. If the moisture is trapped against the knife, it will eventually start to show signs of corrosion and ultimately rust. This is true even with stainless steels or well-oiled carbon steels. Many knife collectors will have dedicated containers or display cabinets used to store their knives. Some knife owners will even use moisture-regulating containers and devices.

A cheap and easy way to store a knife is to first dedicate a drawer or a sealable bin to your knives or outdoor equipment. You can store your knife right beside its sheath, but it's pretty dangerous to leave a blade uncovered. The last thing you want is to reach in without looking and end up with a knife through your hand. To avoid this, it's perfectly okay to lightly wrap the blade once or twice with a very **breathable cotton material**. To make things even safer, you can use **cardboard** and **tape** to create a slipcover for the blade. Along with properly storing a blade, always remember to apply a light coat of oil on the surface of the steel after use and prior to storing.

KNIFEMAKING TERMS

Belly: The curved portion of a blade designed for slicing. Also known as a sweep.

Bevel: The tapered part of the blade that extends from the spine down to the cutting edge.

Block: A squared-up piece of material used to create a knife handle. This is an individual piece that can be split down the middle to create scales or used alone to accept a hidden tang.

Butt: The end of a knife's handle.

Choil: The unsharpened portion of the blade's edge that is close to the handle. Some choils are notched to help aid in sharpening.

Clip Point: A common blade shape characterized by a spine with a front section that appears to be clipped off. This front section can either be straight or concave and results in a fine point.

Cold Shut: Also known as a lap or fold. A defect that forms whenever metal folds over itself during forging.

Decarburization: The removal of carbon from the surface of the steel as a result of heating in a medium that reacts with the carbon. Decarburization is usually present to a slight extent in steel forgings. Excessive decarburization can result in defective products.

Drawing: A forging operation in which the cross section of forging stock is reduced and the stock is lengthened.

Drop Point: A common blade shape characterized by a convex spine the curves down from the handle to the point. This creates an easily controlled point and a bigger belly for slicing.

Flattening: The forging operation of flattening the stock prior to further working.

Forging: The process of working metal to a desired shape by impact or pressure with hammers, forging machines, presses, rolls, and related forming equipment.

Grain: An individual crystal in a polycrystalline metal or alloy.

Guard: Part of the handle designed to prevent the hand from slipping up onto the blade.

Heat-Treating: A group of metalworking processes used to alter the physical properties of steel.

Heat Treat: A sequence of controlled heating and cooling operations applied to a solid metal to impart desired properties.

Jimping: A notched portion of the spine, often close to the handle, designed for improved grip.

Micro Bevel: Also known as a "secondary bevel," a micro bevel is a very small bevel created at the very edge of a blade. Micro bevels strengthen the overall cutting edge.

Pommel: A fitting (commonly made from metal) secured to the butt end of a knife handle.

Quenching: The process in which steel is hardened or strengthened. Quenching often consists of plunging heated steel into a liquid medium such as oil.

Ricasso: The flat and unsharpened portion of the blade between the handle and the bevel.

Scale (Mill Scale): The heavy oxide layer that forms during heating and forging of steel.

Scales: A prepared style of handle material designed for use on a full-tang knife handle. Scales are often made by cutting a block down its center to create two equal halves.

Smith: The blacksmith, forger, or pressman.

Spear Point: A symmetrical blade shape with a point that's in-line with the center of the knife. Commonly used for throwing knives.

Spine: The unsharpened "back" or "top" of a knife. The spine is the side opposite the sharp edge. Double-edged knives do not have spines.

Stock: The material to be forged regardless of form. Also, an individual piece of metal used to produce a single forging.

Swedge: Also known as "false edge," this is a portion of the knife's spine that is unsharpened but has been ground to give the appearance that it is sharp.

Tang: The portion of the blade that extends into, and is held by, the handle.

Tanto: Inspired by short swords that were worn by Samurai in feudal Japan, this blade shape replaces a curved belly for an angular edge transition that makes for a much stronger and prominent point.

Tempering: Heating a blade to a non-critical temperature in order to slightly soften the steel. Tempering is used to relieve stresses in steel caused by quenching.

Upset Forging: (1) A forging made by upsetting an appropriate length of bar, billet, or bloom. **(2)** Working metal to increase the cross-sectional area of a portion or all of the stock. **(3)** A forging formed by heading or gathering the material by pressure upon hot or cold metal between dies operated in a horizontal plane.

Sources:
https://gearpatrol.com/2018/09/21/knife-terms/
https://www.forging.org/glossary-of-forging-terms/

APPENDIX: MY SETUP

My personal, ideal setup for basic knifemaking would include the following tools and materials:

- ☐ propane forge
- ☐ anvil
- ☐ cross peen hammer
- ☐ wolf jaw and box jaw tongs
- ☐ quenching container and canola oil
- ☐ tempering oven
- ☐ belt grinder with a variety of ceramic belts
- ☐ angle grinder with cutoff and grinding discs

- ☐ drill press with cobalt and brad-point drill bits
- ☐ center punch
- ☐ single-cut file
- ☐ cabinet rasp, clamps
- ☐ 24-hour epoxy
- ☐ boiled linseed oil and beeswax-based paste (for wood handle finishing)
- ☐ wet-dry sandpaper
- ☐ whetstone

- ☐ leather strop
- ☐ ceramic rod
- ☐ painter's tape
- ☐ markers
- ☐ wax paper
- ☐ towels

Index

Photo Credits

Shutterstock: Anatolir (54 left buff the blade icon); CCinar (24 middle right); Dan Kosmayer (30 top left); design56 (25 bottom right, 168 bottle); donatas1205 (24 bottom right, 162 bottom right); Enlightened Media (19 bottom right); EstudiosOMH (168 toothbrush); Gavran333 (24 top left, 81 left, 161 top right); HADI_TRESNANTAN (54 bottom left leather icon); indigolotos (21 top right); Jiang Zhongyan (161 middle right); jps (17 bottom); Khamkhlai Thanet (23 top right); NikolayN (63); notsuperstar (24 bottom left); photopia90 (21 top left); PodPad (19 top left); preedee anantuntikul (23 bottom right); Rvector (55 vise icons); valzan (51 bottom); xpixel (58 bottom); Yuriy Redkin (20 bottom right)

ABOUT THE AUTHOR

Brad Richardson was born and raised in Illinois but now resides in northern Michigan. He is an avid outdoorsman and pulls much of his inspiration from his time spent in the wilderness. Brad has worked on multiple wilderness survival projects with the History Channel, taking him from Canada to Mongolia and forcing him to rely on his primitive skill sets and handmade knives. The knife is an essential tool for any outdoorsman, and over the years Brad has developed a good understanding of knife functionality.

Prior to making knives, he spent a number of years making furniture, which led to his gathering some blacksmithing tools to eventually forge his own furniture hardware. This helped to show him his way around the anvil and some of the other tools used to make knives.

So, with a simple understanding of the tools and overall knife functionality, he began making custom knives in 2014. This was his way to make up for the cheap production knives he'd been using during his outdoor retreats.

Brad has spent recent years training and learning from other bladesmiths, with a focus on the ancient art of Damascus steel. He runs a YouTube channel, sharing blacksmithing and knifemaking content with thousands of subscribers. Brad is a member of the American Bladesmith Society and the founder of Timberlee Tool & Trade.